Channeling the Fray:
Another Side of Privilege

A POETIC MEMOIR BY:

Jennifer Lee Hourin

Hourin House Press
New Jersey

Hourin House
www.hourinhouse.com

Copyright © 2023 by Jennifer Lee Hourin

Printed in the United States of America

All rights reserved. In accordance with the U.S. Copyright Act of 1976, the scanning, uploading, and electronic sharing of any part of this book without the permission of the publisher constitutes unlawful piracy and theft of the author's intellectual property. No part of this book may be reprinted or reproduced in any fashion without the express written permission in writing from the publishers.

Cover illustration by Nicholas J. Hourin

Library of Congress Cataloging-in-Publication Data

Hourin, Jennifer L, 1975-
Channeling the Fray: Another Side of Privilege
A Poetic Memoir
ISBN: 979-8-218-22468-4

Preface

The horrific killing of Mr. George Floyd on May 25, 2020 made an indelible mark on individuals who found themselves understandably enraged, hurt, disillusioned, and otherwise at a great loss for how a white police officer, Derek Chauvin, could so callously and collectedly kneel with full force on the neck of man who was clearly in a state of trauma and distress.[1] For a nation that had experienced the terrifying deaths of Black men such as Trayvon Martin,[2] Michael Brown,[3] Eric Garner,[4] and more, at the hands of either law enforcement officers or those attempting to act in such a vain, the murder of George Floyd was, in many ways, a final straw. It was for me. I can only imagine with the most searing part of my soul, and the deepest rhythm of my heart, how it must have felt for anyone Black to have witnessed the killing of George Floyd in person, on television, or video camera. What I can do, however, is tell the story of how this murder affected this white person, who grew up around the block from a housing project in a working poor ghetto, and experienced being physically held down, without the ability to breathe, and nearly killed by authorities who never recognized my state of trauma. I can also weigh in on the dialogue around white privilege, which in many ways is more complicated than a sound bite can suggest. My goal is to encourage deeper understanding and empathy across lines of race, ethnicity, gender, class, and place.

Specifically, in this work I share a perspective of what it was like to grow up on a "border block" that separated the largely Italian American section from the largely African American section in Marion, Jersey City. I detail some of the difficult situations that emerged during the 1970s, 1980s, and 1990s when Jersey City experienced significant out-migration of the middle class[5] along with the influx of illicit drugs,[6] the loss of decent paying blue-collar

---

[1] Evan, H. et. al (2020). How George Floyd Was Killed in Police Custody. *The New York Times*.

[2] Palmer, Ph.D., G. L. (2013). Dissecting the killing of Trayvon Martin: The power factor. *Journal for Social Action in Counseling & Psychology, 5*(1), 126–130.

[3] Suggs, E. (2015). The Michael Brown killing: What you need to know. *The Atlanta Journal- Constitution*.

[4] Sanburn, J. (2014). Behind the Video of Eric Garner's Deadly Confrontation With New York Police. *TIME Magazine*. Retrieved from https://time.com/3016326/eric-garner-video-police-chokehold-death/.

[5] Wilson, W. J. (2012). *The Truly Disadvantaged: The Inner City, the Underclass, and Public Policy*. University of Chicago Press. See also Wilson, W. J. (1991). Another look at the truly disadvantaged. *Political Science Quarterly, 106*(4), 639-656.

[6] Weisburd, D., & Green, L. (1995). Policing drug hot spots: The Jersey City drug market analysis experiment. *Justice Quarterly, 12*(4), 711-735. See also Mazerolle, L. G., Ready,

manufacturing positions,[7] and the rise of mass incarceration,[8] mental health issues,[9] and environmental challenges, including toxic waste sites.[10]

As one of the most diverse cities in the world,[11] Jersey City presents an important case study for understanding the development of intergroup relationships within a ghetto. In this work, I reference tensions among African Americans and Italian Americans and the police and explain how many of the anti-Black assaults in Jersey City were predated by anti-Italian assaults, and how insinuations of "Black blood" among Italians were used to incite violence.[12] I begin to explain carefully how some Mafia figures stepped in to ameliorate racial tensions and create a kind of social order within Marion, Jersey City. Other Mafia figures, by virtue of maintaining a schizophrenic culture, made racial tensions worse. The rules regarding race were complicated, yet nuanced. Sometimes children of different groups were allowed to play together; other times they were not. Many African Americans on the Italian side of Marion were also Italian. Racial challenges took place along Broadway, the path children

---

J., Terrill, W., & Waring, E. (2000). Problem-oriented policing in public housing: The Jersey City evaluation. *Justice Quarterly, 17*(1), 129-158.

[7] Wilson, W. J. (2011). *When Work Disappears: The World of the New Urban Poor*. Vintage.

[8] Clear, T. R. (2009). *Imprisoning Communities: How Mass Incarceration Makes Disadvantaged Neighborhoods worse*. Oxford University Press.

[9] Breggin, P. R. (1994). *Toxic Psychiatry: Why Therapy, Empathy and Love Must Replace the Drugs, Electroshock, and Biochemical Theories of the" New Psychiatry"*. Macmillan. See also Smith, D. E. (1990). *The Conceptual Practices of Power: A Feminist Sociology of Knowledge*. University of Toronto Press. See also Swartz, S. (1999). IV. Lost Lives: Gender, History and Mental Illness in the Cape, 1891-1910. *Feminism & Psychology, 9*(2), 152-158.

[10] Stern, A. H., Gochfeld, M., & Lioy, P. J. (2013). Two decades of exposure assessment studies on chromate production waste in Jersey City, New Jersey—what we have learned about exposure characterization and its value to public health and remediation. *Journal of Exposure Science & Environmental Epidemiology, 23*(1), 2-12.

[11] Zeitlinger, R. (2022). This New Jersey City is Still the Most Ethnically Diverse in the Entire Country. *The Jersey Journal*.

[12] Mayor Frank Hague was the Democratic Mayor of Jersey City from 1917 to 1947. He is said to have ruled Jersey City with an "iron-fist." As the son of Irish immigrants, Mayor Hague appeared to succumb to the Irish-Italian conflict of his day. He held disgust for Italians, whose "dark, swarthy complexion" earned them the name "dago." An extraordinarily corrupt regime, Mayor Hague would use the police force to go on searches for Italian men. For more information on Mayor Frank Hague, please see Vernon, L. F. (2011). *The Life & Times of Jersey City Mayor Frank Hague: I am the Law*. Arcadia Publishing. Also see Raffety, M. (2009). Political Ethics and Public Style in the Early Career of Jersey City's Frank Hague. *New Jersey History, 124*(1), 29-56. For more information on how Italians were subjugated under Irish folks, please see Vecoli, R. J. (1969). Prelates and peasants: Italian immigrants and the Catholic church. *Journal of Social History*, 217-268. See also Barrett, J. R., & Roediger, D. R. (2005). The Irish and the "Americanization" of the" New Immigrants" in the Streets and in the Churches of the Urban United States, 1900-1930. *Journal of American Ethnic History, 24*(4), 3-33.

walked to go to school and to Journal Square, the city's central business district. As an insider, I provide fresh insight into Dr. Anderson's powerful work on the code of the street[13] and campaigns for territorial control.[14]

Moreover, this story explains what happened when a Jersey City girl makes an attempt at upward mobility by attending Rutgers University in New Brunswick for undergraduate degrees in Criminal Justice and Psychology with a minor in Sociology. The years at Rutgers, 93-97, illustrate the experience of being one of only a few white students in both the Equal Opportunity Fund (EOF), a program to help underprivileged students adjust to life at college, and the Ronald E. Mc Nair Post-Baccalaureate program, designed to help prepare traditionally underrepresented students for graduate studies. The on and off years at Yale University 1997-2009 illustrate how it felt to be continually asked "where are you from?" because of one's accent, and to be told to forget about one's working-class roots or any ideas of applying theory to poverty, as that was considered "non-academic." It also reveals what it meant to lead an ethnographic study of mostly Egyptian Muslims in Jersey City whose lives were turned around as a result of 9/11. Local Muslims came under intense scrutiny because the 1993 World Trade Center was said to have been planned from a Mosque in Jersey City.[15] This work reveals what it feels like to be accused of being a suicide bomber, to have the police invade one's home searching for signs of allegiance to Muslim extremism, and to end up in mental health facilities as a result of trauma. Throughout this story I illustrate how strong women of all backgrounds served as mentors in what became a very tumultuous life experience. While there is currently important attention on understanding the systemic effects of critical topics such as racism,[16] I lift up the hidden social interactions that show how people with varying levels of power use their positions to overpower, hurt, and undermine those they wish to humiliate and control.[17] I also problematize Psychiatry for misunderstanding cultural trauma and the supernatural.

This book fits within many genres. As a book of poems, it clearly fits within a kind of dark genre of poetry. Indeed, the vast majority of this book is written from the voice of a little girl who is sad. However, there are parts of this book that may strike one as angry or even paranoid. These poems are important

---

[13] Anderson, E. (2000). *Code of the Street: Decency, Violence, and the Moral Life of the Inner City*. WW Norton & Company.

[14] Suttles, G. D. (1968). *The Social Order of the Slum: Ethnicity and Territory in the Inner City*. University of Chicago Press.

[15] Bryan, J. (2005). Constructing "the true Islam" in hostile times: The impact of 9/11 on Arab Muslims in Jersey City. *Wounded City: The Social Impact of 911*, 133-162.

[16] Feagin, J. (2013). *Systemic Racism: A Theory of Oppression*. Routledge.

[17] For an excellent discussion on healing the "victim within" and "oppressor within," please see Hooks, B. (1989). *Talking Back: Thinking Feminist, Thinking Black* (Vol. 10). South End Press.

for illustrating that the process of healing trauma can be complicated and messy, and not always happy and uplifting. *Channeling the Fray*, in my humble opinion, is a process that allows one to get in touch with feelings, visions, and experiences that live within the fringe of one's mind. Releasing these feelings, I believe, is needed to help heal trauma.

As a memoir, this book can be used to help individuals seeking to heal from trauma and mental health issues as well as community-based organizations that run programs to help those experiencing issues of poverty, job insecurity, racism, mental health, substance use, familial incarceration, homelessness, and beyond. This book could easily be added to syllabi or curricula toward the goal of healing from what are called Adverse Childhood Experiences (ACES).[18] I can envision state agencies and community-based organizations that specialize in child welfare using this book to help train staff on what children go through as well as sharing it with youth who are facing similar challenges. Police departments could benefit from understanding more about the inner-workings of trauma,[19] gaslighting,[20] and the cycle of violence.[21] I can also imagine this work being used to enhance all of the powerful and important work on Diversity, Equity, and Inclusion (DEI) by including the "lived experiences" of those in the working class who face challenges of relative poverty, domestic violence, and trauma despite being considered "white."

In addition, this book can fit within a body of work that is critical of the status quo. This work makes many critical commentaries about the tendency of political leaders on the left and the right to divide the working class and the way that race can be manipulated in that endeavor. It also critiques academics for being petty and casting out the role of ethnicity for white Americans through many scholarly works without ever trying to truly understand it.[22] This work aims to show what white ethnics have in common with people of color. It also alludes to rumors about the Skull and Bones secret society at Yale University,[23]

---

[18] Whiteside-Mansell, L., McKelvey, L., Saccente, J., & Selig, J. P. (2019). Adverse childhood experiences of urban and rural preschool children in poverty. *International Journal of Environmental Research and Public Health, 16*(14), 2623. See also Giovanelli, A., Reynolds, A. J., Mondi, C. F., & Ou, S. R. (2016). Adverse childhood experiences and adult well-being in a low-income, urban cohort. *Pediatrics, 137*(4).

[19] Erikson, K. (1991). Notes on trauma and community. *American Imago, 48*(4), 455-472.

[20] Sweet, P. L. (2019). The sociology of gaslighting. *American Sociological Review, 84*(5), 851-875.

[21] Walker, L. E. (2016). *The Battered Woman Syndrome*. Springer publishing company.

[22] Waters, M. C. (1990). *Ethnic Options: Choosing Identities in America*. Univ of California Press. See also Steinberg, S. (2001). *The Ethnic Myth: Race, Ethnicity, and Class in America*. Beacon Press.

[23] Millegan, K. (Ed.). (2004). *Fleshing out Skull & Bones: Investigations into America's most powerful secret society*. Trine Day. See also Sora, S. (2003). *Secret Societies of America's Elite: From the Knights Templar to Skull and Bones*. Simon and Schuster.

and argues that Antonio Gramsci's prediction that a working-class person who rises to the top of education is seen as an active threat within academia. It likens academia to a cutting game of thrones.[24] Finally, there is a very spiritual component to this work. At times, it appears to channel the very word of God. This work is important for showing how deeply the labeling process hurts.[25] It is also important for raising class-consciousness. This work illustrates a more vulnerable side of whiteness than is typically shared. Sociologists and scholars in Italian American studies, Urban Studies, Psychology, and Race and Ethnic Studies can use this book as a way of adding lived experience to their classes. Finally, through poetry readings and restorative justice circles, I can imagine using this work to heal current tensions around race, class, gender, mental health, ethnicity, immigrant experience, policing, and political bend. I am most hopeful it can be used to heal inter-generational trauma, and break the cycles of inter-generational poverty and mental illness.

---

[24] Gramsci, A. (2011). Prison Notebooks, Volumes 1-3. See also Karabel, J. (1976). See also Revolutionary contradictions: Antonio Gramsci and the problem of intellectuals. *Politics & Society*, *6*(2), 123-172.

[25] Erikson, K. T. (2018). Notes on the sociology of deviance. In *Deviance & Liberty* (pp. 15-23). Routledge. See also Goffman, E. (2009). *Stigma: Notes on the Management of Spoiled Identity*. Simon and Schuster.

Acknowledgement

I owe debts of gratitude to my ancestors that I wish no one to ever bear. My husband and children have reminded me how good it is to still care. Much of my life was spent worrying about all the wrong people. But now that I am old enough, I look out for the steeple. Grampa Charlie was my world and taught me all I know. Nonna Tina inspired me to compete strongly for the show. My parents gave me many lessons, as did my twin sister. But much of my life was set in play by a very big, conniving twister. Granpda Stanley saved my soul along with Uncle Mark. Both men saw me in a cave and rescued me out from the dark. To my children, Angelia and Gianna, I love you more than you know. Always remember Mommy will be with you as you grow. My husband, Nick, you're a fine man whose loyalty has come through. Now, I wish to tell my story and reach out to all of you. I pray it helps to heal some hearts, at least in knowing you're not all alone. I hope one day we can all connect and we won't even need a phone. I thank Marion, Jersey City, NJ for making me so strong. I thank God for entrusting me with this message, and you all for listening to my song. I pray you find it comforting to know how to "write" a wrong. I pray you form a diverse community where we all can truly belong.

Father's Name

When I was five years old
I walked up to Frank's candy store
A bratty girl was there before me
She laughed when I came through the door.

With the meanest look of hell
She gave me the lowest blow
I know your father's real name
Bet you don't cause you're slow.

My father's name is John
I don't need you to tell me that
Your father's name is Gary
She shot back with her bat.

I left the store feeling angered
I went home and told mom the same
She stayed super quiet
When I uttered Gary's name.

That night John came in
And we recited all our prayers
Then he said he had to tell us something
And within me I was scared.

He said "I'm not your real father"
And I bursted out crying
"Are you leaving us?"
Inside I was dying.

He began to cry as well
But quickly cleared his voice
I am still your father
But I am here by choice.

Gary was your biological father
But he left when you were six-months old
That's when I met your mom
And so, the story began to unfold.

Barbie Dream House

The most special present ever
Was a beautiful barbie dream house
My stepfather set up all the furniture
It was tiny enough for a mouse.

I was afraid to touch anything
Afraid it would fall apart
Everything in life was beginning
To tear right into my heart.

My mom and stepfather kept fighting
Mostly over bills
Sometimes it was over me
And all of my clumsy spills.

He began to lose weight
Rapidly he became super slim
I didn't know it was a substance
That caused the change in him.

I could sense the mood before I'd come home
I could feel the chill in the vestibule
Sometimes I'd stay downstairs
And wait an hour after school.

I'd make my way up the stairs
And dig my nails into the thick brown molding
Thinking if I could just reach wood
It would stop my mother's scolding.

But it really never worked
I'd always come in when they were bickering
The lights would get turned off
And mom would start her snickering.

You couldn't pay the bills?
Where is the money going?
He had lost his job
Tried pretending he was still showing.

Born Favored

Growing up as a twin
Was really, really hard
Everyone always compared us
And it left me really scarred.

They'd try to put us in boxes
So, they could tell us apart
They said I had the long face
And my sister took that to heart.

They referred to her as round face
And sometimes called her "fat"
Even though I was just a few pounds less
I escaped that name-calling tat.

I was also pretty lucky
I'd win raffles and all kinds of prizes
My family started to think
I had a secret gift for surprises.

The happiest day of my young life
Was when I won a gymnastics trophy
I landed a perfect forward flip
And ended with three splits done slowly.

But they felt bad for my sister
She didn't always win
They started to say it was unfair
And I was Gary's daughter with sin.

My mom wanted to call me Alexis
After my big Uncle Al
But Gary said you already named one
So, he took on the role of pal.

I never felt comfortable with my name
Though it was popular and savored
My family saw me as the lucky one
Said it was unfair I was born favored.

Car Door

At around the age of seven
My hand was slammed in a car door
Was it to try to secure funding?
To lift the family from being poor?

Or was it out of hatred?
For being another's daughter?
Named by another man?
Munchausen syndrome[26] was the order?

"You're probably gonna lose those fingers"
Is what was said to me
But I wrapped them in tissue paper
And held them tighter than can be.

And when we arrived at the ER
The doctor was amazed
What happened to your hand?
"It's a miracle," he praised.

A miracle heard the changed man
And it happened to her?
Guess I need a new plot
To get back at Jennifer.

And so, the plot became driving me crazy
Telling everyone I was bad
And in the process of doing so
I really did become quite mad.

They began telling me I was violent
I kicked my sister out of the womb
I gave her a red mark on her head
And I belonged in a tomb.

---

[26] Meadow, R. (1989). ABC of child abuse. Munchausen syndrome by proxy. *BMJ: British Medical Journal, 299*(6693), 248.

Well, years went by and this carried on
Mom blamed me for missing the lottery
Said I distracted her from picking the winning numbers
Made me beg for money with pottery.

What a tree.

Please Don't

I'm crouched in the closet
Hiding for fear
Dreading the hour
When Mr. Henry comes near.

I'm a very bad girl
That is for sure
I deserve to be beaten
Until I am sore.

Then comes the moment
I've seen it before
The moment he finds
What he had been looking for.

That look in his eye
A keen evil stare
Like that of a fox
Before attacking a hare.

Daddy, please don't
I want just to plead
But I know it's useless
He'd still proceed.

Run-in

I was a very light sleeper
And one night it came in handy
I was sleeping in the bed with my twin sister
Something woke me up in a dandy.

I walked into the kitchen
And looked at the door knob
Someone was jimmying it
And it caused my heart to throb.

I couldn't touch the door knob
I was entranced in the moment
Then it stopped moving
And I knew I had only a second to slow it.

I still couldn't touch it
It was like it was hot
So, I gained my composure
And screamed in a stern voice to stop the plot.

I said "Uh, Dad" very assuredly
To let him think he would be toast
It worked like a charm
The dude left before I was roast.

Then another time
There was a prowler on the roof
Uncle Alex yelled "get down low"
On the floor we fell in a poof.

Then Uncle Mark got his shotgun
And went outside
His dog, Bambi, went after the police officer
Who nearly took her life.

The cop pointed the gun at Bambi
And Uncle Mark cocked up
Said you shoot her, you're a dead man
The dude lowered his gun away from the pup.

As this was happening,
The prowler got away
Cops and Italians always fought
It was never "ok."

Not too long after
All of a sudden
Someone stole Bambi
Most likely the cop for the "run-in."

School Ground

One day at lunch
Daddy John came to the school ground
He was in his work uniform
He was talking almost without sound.

He looked at me carefully
And said in a serious tone
"I have to go away for a while
But you could come with me on the road."

I looked at him
And didn't know what to say
Was he trying to kidnap me?
Or take me away?

Was he trying to save me?
From a hard life?
I knew my mom was tough
But thought we all could survive.

I just wanted them together
Although they fought that much
I didn't know which one to choose
My stomach was ill from the sucker punch.

But at the end of the day
I chose to stay with mom
Something in his eyes was different
And it caused me alarm.

So, when it came time meet him
At three o'clock
I cried my heart out in a pillow
And let my soul rock.

Cheryl

I stayed in Grampa's room
Cause he worked the night shift
Nonna made a bed out of the couch
They came through in a jiff.

My mom couldn't keep us then
She became a nervous single-mom
My stepfather got hooked on cocaine
And left us like a bomb.

He spent the money on drugs
And we soon got evicted
Had to find rooms real fast
But the block was really twisted.

It went from being a wonderful place
With kids playing on the street
Nonnas would keep an eye on us
And watch out for the creep.

There was some racial division
But only cause big eyes were on the prowl
I lived around the block from the projects
And it really shaped my growl.

My Uncle Louie lived in the projects
And he went to jail
He was "built" and good looking
Very popular with "female tail."

I used to look out the back fire-escape room window
And wonder why my stepfather left
I remember one day waiting for him
A prayer with every breath.

I went outside on a land lady's stoop
And waited all day long
Each car that came down the street
I jumped up and sang a song.

Here he is, this must be him
That is what I said
But he never showed up
Mom came out and said he must be dead.

Up in apartment seven at 71 Wallis
When my life was in peril
I'd always look to the girls in the projects
And found one whom I'll call Cheryl.

She had pretty beads in her braids
And I asked mom to do my hair the same
But she said they'd say I'm a "wanna be"
And that it's a Black and white game.

Still, I'd look to Cheryl
And she'd look to me
And then I'd see the car
Her mom worked as a night lady.

I thought my life couldn't get any worse
And then our neighbor would start his yelling
I'd hear him through paper-thin walls
And feel broker than Janet Yellen.

I wanted to help my friend, Joe
Because I knew he knew I heard
But there was nothing we could do at the time
The neighborhood was becoming absurd.

Public service shut the jobs down
And my family wasn't educated
My biological father left at six-months old
He saw my family as tainted.

Gary's mother was described as a very cold German
The "Bryans" lived in an upper-middle-class suburb
Didn't care for our project-neighborhood
Would've rather their son kick my mom to the curb.

Gary's mother demanded an abortion
But Nonna fought right back
If you try to kill any baby
You'll be down for attack.

My nonna didn't play
When it came to matters of the heart
Though she'd cry on the bed everyday
Being tough was her part.

One day Gary's mother came to visit
Nonna said I did something really terrific
She asked his mother if she saw "how smart?"
But I didn't pass the sniff test.

At that moment, Nonna picked me up
She lifted me to the sky
"Let them be achievers!" She exclaimed
Her prayer came through like pie.

Caught

Uncle Mark had a heart of gold
But more than that he was fair
He once asked an African American Italian teen
To look after me with care.

Frankie came up to me on Broadway
And said your Uncle Mark told me to watch you
You have any problem with anyone
You let me know, and I'll handle the fool.

Uncle Mark was raised to be strong
Nonna Tina didn't play
When he was young there was a bully
Scaring everyone away.

Uncle Mark came in sick
Told Nonna Tina about the boy
She said "get out there and fight him"
She was anything but coy.

He said "I can't, he's too big"
And Nonna said "oh yeah"
She grabbed a broom
And held it tight in the air.

She said if you don't go out there
And fight that little brat
Then you'll have to fight your mother
He wasn't prepared for that.

"Ma, I can't fight you
You're my mother"
She said "thems the breaks"
And dared him with her piercing eye-plunder.

He went outside and
Said to the kid
My mom said I have to fight you
He was prepared to be licked.

But to his surprise
Uncle Mark won that fight
He beat up the bully
And it became the source of his pride.

Later on, in life
When female cousins had problems with men
He would find a way to make them disappear
For someone going through domestic violence, he was Heaven-sent.

I know this will come out wrong
But I have to tell you
What happened to Mr. George Floyd
Was also a Marion venue.

Marion Italians and African Americans
Didn't have the ability to record the police in action
Trained never to give away motives
But that doesn't mean they backed down.

Marion men waited many years
Found creative ways to meet up with certain cops
Knelt on their stomachs
Until their breathing stopped.

They would do this in private
So as not to invoke public eyes or complain
Marion believed it was most important
To free the spirit and then go on and maintain.

But I know the Justice system
Has changed a lot
I've been teaching it for many years
And can really call all the shots.

Still, I stay low
Like I was taught
Hoping one day you'll catch up
Before my secret is caught.

Macaroni and Meatballs

Although much of childhood was sad
I found many things to make me smile
One was Sunday dinner at Nonna's
Macaroni and meatballs for the child.

We would all pack into her apartment
Extended cousins, uncles, and aunts
Everyone was welcome
We'd cram in like a tight pair of pants.

The kids would play outside
As the grown-ups gambled with cards
Sometimes we were allowed to join in
If we were blocked out of the yards.

You could smell dinner from outside
Walking home from Church
You could taste the sauce and meatballs
It made you feel good in a lurch.

When my stepfather returned from being away
Grandpa Stanley would also come over
We'd watch football games
And polish mom's eggplant Chevy Nova.

Grandpa Stanley was Polish
But he loved Italian food
Almost married an Italian woman
But he got drafted, and she gave him the boot.

He was a very good baseball player
And probably could have gone pro
But the war in Germany took a toll on him
Even if he didn't say so.

Still, at the end of the day
We'd watch "Murder She Wrote"[27]
It was one way we all bonded
And it helped me become a poet.

---

[27] Lansburg, A., Fischer, P.S., Levinson, R., Link, W., & Moessinger, D. (Executive Producers). (1984-1996). *Murder She Wrote* [TV series]. CBS.

Roy Rogers

When I was little
Going to the park was a treat
I'd wait for Grampa to take me
He was always so sweet.

He'd come by in the morning
Cause he worked the night shift
He was a boiler man
And he carried no rift.

He'd extend out his hand
And say just this
"Do you want the jingly stuff or the paper?"
And I'd smile with sis.

He'd give me money for candy
And I'd always choose the change
Cause he'd give more than a dollar
So that I could rearrange.

I'd always buy my mom
A necklace for a dollar
I tried to make her smile
Help her work in cruel white-collar.

Sometimes I would have
An extra 50 cents
I'd buy some candy
Or save it for the rent.

But it was cause of Grampa
I'd smile inside
He just made me feel wholesome
And gave me my pride.

We used to go to Roy Rogers
They had a bar with the fixins
We'd sit outside in the car
And start reminiscing.

We'd play the bird game
And it went like this
I'm thinking of a bird
And the others would guess.

We didn't have jumpy houses
Or a big splash park
But Grampa always found a way
To bring my spirit out from the dark.

And once in a while
Grampa would even take me to Kmarts
Let me pick out a toy
And buy me some sweet tarts.

He was the greatest grampa
He filled my whole heart
With him by my side
I always felt I was part.

Nonna

Nonna worked as a chaperone
On a school bus for kids with special needs
She'd always buy them coats during winter
We couldn't sleep thinking they'd freeze.

Some kids could not sit still
And she'd get them headphones with music
That would keep them happy
And they wouldn't feel so useless.

They'd sing to her on the bus
And it would make everyone feel good
Her driver became a close friend
He'd pick Nonna up in the hood.

Nonna didn't drive
At the time the whole family had one car
Nonna was one of few white workers
Her dyed red-hair stood out on the tar.

Nonna's Black friends took up for her
And said she was their "girl"
This way no one would step to her
Her hair was a tight short curl.

Then when she retired
Grampa drove her and Miss Joan around
Miss Joan's son once went outside
To give Miss Tina a pound.

Though he was shocked she was white
He knew that something was sound
They were always there in a jiff
And they took his mom around town.

I wish my mom had a similar story
But hers was really twisted
She was not liked by any ladies
Most likely because of her image.

Piccirilli

My nonna was born in 1927
She was one of seven kids
Eleven if you count stillborns
My family always did.

She was a scrawny young girl
Cause food was hard to find
The kids made fun of her name, Piccirilli
They made her die inside.

The kids would say "pinch a penny, piss a penny"
And throw pennies at her feet
She would pick them up with a low face
Knowing she could buy a small treat.

She idolized her father
But Italian was not allowed in sight
The family had to learn English
Whether or not it was right.

They had slave owners in Italy
They were called "The Padrone"[28]
Money made had to go back to them
Lest they killed your family back home.

But you all look to Italian immigrants
And think we've had it easy
Never thinking we're only trying to move up
Just like George and Weezy.[29]

I wish I could take those little brats
Who picked on my nonna
I wish I could make them eat their words
Make them feel her low, ah.

---

[28] Jalongo, M. R. (2008). "Little Italian Slaves": Lessons Learned from the Padrone Boys. *Early Childhood Education Journal*, 36(3), 209-212. See also Iorizzo, L. J. (1966). *Italian immigration and the impact of the padrone system*. Syracuse University.

[29] Duclon, D., Leavitt, R., Moriarty, J., Milligan, M., Nicholl, D., Ross, M., Sunga, G., & West, B. (Executive Producers). (1975-1985) *The Jeffersons* [TV Series]. CBS.

But instead, I must compose myself
And pretend those things didn't happen
After all we've been told white ethnicity
Is a tall tale that flies high like a falcon.

Italian Charade

One day we went to Hoboken
To pick up pastry from Carlo's[30]
It was long before he got famous
We all waited in the car, close.

Grampa went in
To get what Nonna needed on the shelf
Inside the car I could hear her talking
She often had conversations with herself.

"Bet she's smart" is what she said
She uttered it under her breath
It was a petite blonde woman with a fancy coat
Nonna looked at her and felt like death.

Nonna graduated the 8th grade
And she was very proud of that fact
But it wasn't always easy
Schools said Italians didn't know how to act.[31]

I felt bad to see Nonna so low like stinky trash
I directed my anger toward the blonde woman
Though she didn't do anything wrong
I wanted to sign Nonna up for Kumon.

Nonna felt really insecure
About her immigrant upbringing
She'd often talk about her parents
Her voice was hurt and ringing.

She once wanted to smell like her father
So, she got up on a chair
She tried to get his cologne down from a shelf
But it smashed all into her hair.

---

[30] Feeley, S., Berger, J., Valastro, B., & Edward, A. (Executive Producers). (2009-2020). *Cake Boss* [TV series]. TLC, Discovery Family.

[31] Covello, L. (1945). The Sociological Background of the Italo-American School Child: A Study of the Southern Italian Family Mores and Their Effect on the School Situation in Italy and America. *New York*.

She ended up with stitches on her head
And her father wasn't happy
She just wanted to be like him
He was a dapper man, never scrappy.

He spent his money on suits and hats
To ensure the people's respect
He used to take Nonna out to eat
To make her feel like an empress.

He never had all the money
But developed a clever scam
He sent back the food three quarters into it
And said "don't insult me with your lamb!"

He said this to warrant a discount
And that is a family trait
If ever you want your kids to feel special
Just take them out—don't let them wait!

He maintained his stature and
Everyone thought he was made
Though he worked at Public Service
He championed this Italian charade.

Chantilly Lace

Back in the day
Italians and Irish didn't get along
Then Nonna met Grampa
He was told he was Irish with scorn.

Growing up in the South
Grampa was told his mother was Irish
And that was a "dig"
Through DNA we learned she was actually English.

But, in any case
When it came time for Nonna to introduce Grampa
She told her father he was Irish
And he wasn't a happy camper.

He said "no Irish in this house"
Cause many of them were cops
But then he agreed to meet Grampa
And his heart almost stopped.

He took one look at Grampa
And he was in love
He saw right through his skin
And met a white dove.

Grampa's smile was so wholesome
Who wouldn't want him for his daughter's mate?
There was no one more gentle
For within him was not one ounce of hate.

Nonna's brothers also loved him
Though they hazed him a bit
Grampa did more for their father
Than they ever did.

Grampa used to help him crush the grapes
And make the homemade wine
Grampa took him to the doctors
And all over Newark to find the right vine.

Pop took Grampa under his wing
Got him a job at Public Service
Treated him better than a son
And not because he was nervous.

Grampa had a heart
The heart of "the one"
He loved his new Italian family
Pop Piccirilli called him "son."

Pop told him: "son, what you see
You don't see.
What you hear, you don't hear."

Pop was schooling him to the code
The code of the streets
He never read an academic book
But lived it on his feet.

He used to prophesize to Nonna
"One day, you'll see Black power
Hoboken will be built up"
That was long before any towers.

The truth is he wanted Black people
To put the "Medigans" in their place
He felt it was their time
To throw it in "their face."

But some wouldn't know that side of Italians
Because it doesn't show them as disgraced
Some only seem to like stories
That demonize people by race.

Chantilly Lace.[32]

---

[32] Yellen, L. (Director) (1993). *Chantilly Lace* [Film]. Sony Pictures.

Cousins

One of the happiest times of childhood
Was when my little cousin was born
I told all my friends at school
She was to be adored.

We used to drive up to Cliffside
On a Friday night
We'd watch our little cousin
And Nonna wouldn't be so uptight.

She could let her hair down
And all we'd do was laugh
Nonna's niece was like a trucker
She'd put you in a comical trance.

On the way back home
We'd sit in the back of Grampa's car
Our heads faced the rear traffic
And we'd sing some Donna Summer.

"On the Radio"[33] was our favorite
Cause it started slow and then sped up
Grampa smiled so wholesomely
The car was about to erupt.

These were the simple happy times
The ones I cherish so much
When I begin to get mad at life
I think of them in a clutch.

---

[33] Summer, D., & Moroder, G. (1979). On the Radio [Recorded by Donna Summer]. On. *On the Radio: Greatest Hits Vol. I & II* [Album]. Casablanca.

Alpine

One time Daddy John got a car
And he took us all over
We used to go to Alpine, NJ
And drive through the town so sober.

We went to look at houses
And dream of one we'd like to buy
"This one is mine, Daddy!"
We'd laugh and look up to the sky.

It was a way of dreaming
But inside Daddy John was sad
He played the lottery religiously
And wondered why God didn't grow his pad.

He began to lose his religion
After teaching it all to us
He began to lose heart
That Jesus would come and save us.

I wanted to look in his eyes
And say "Dad, I got what you need"
But he tried impressing my mother
With all kinds of material greed.

She demanded a fur coat
And jewelry all abound
No one could keep up with her
Not even the one once crowned.

I don't know why she wanted clothes
All I wanted was cheer
For me and Grampa a card game was it
We'd laugh throughout the year.

But my mom was a different kind
She wanted to be idolized
It took me many years
But I found a way to break through the lies.

Tree House

We went up to the Poconos
With a friend from school
My parents came too
It was all really cool.

They had some old bikes
And a full Olympic pool
We got to relay race
And act like a fool.

A boy had a tree house
And it was really fun
I climbed to the top
Wanted to reach the sun.

Then the boy gave me a dare
See if you can jump down
I looked at the distance
And prayed a prayer without sound.

I put my hands behind me
And imagined a pole
I held onto it tightly
And it helped me drop slow.

I landed on my feet
And everyone was amazed
Then my sister stood up
And wanted to try the same.

But when she came down
She fell flat on her belly
I ran around her in circles
We didn't have any cellie.

Someone ran to my parents
And, of course, they blamed me
Why'd you make her jump
From high off the tree?

"I didn't make her
She wanted to try"
But I didn't say anymore
I just swallowed my sigh.

White Van

One day in the morning
On my walk to school
A white van pulled over on Broadway
And opened the door real cool.

He extended his hand out
And had a picture of my stepfather
He asked "do you know this man?"
But inside my mind screamed "monster."

I shot him back a hard look
And said "I don't know you"
The Italian Nonnas were looking on
So, there was nothing he could do.

I shoulder-punched my way to school that day
Giving him the keen old stare
I didn't run and I'm proud of that
But I certainly walked fast out of scare.

Holy Ghost

I was an altar server at Church
And one day something happened
I was holding the golden plate
When the host flew out of its cabin.

It landed on the floor
And the Priest got really nervous
He said a special prayer
And blessed the entire service.

After that, going to Church
Was a little different
I'd always genuflect and bow
But the Priest looked at me with reverence.

When it was my time to receive
He'd ask "body of Christ?"
With a question mark at the end
My look was one of surprise.

I just nodded and said "amen"
Though I didn't know what it meant
I started to feel unsettled
Like they wanted me to pay some rent.

I would often close my eyes
When it came my time to receive
I felt they blamed me for the host
And I was looking for reprieve.

Jesus

Way back in grammar school
The teachers would say
Jesus can be anyone
So always remember to pray.

Jesus can be in this room
Jesus can be in this class
Jesus will need our help
Remember to go to mass.

Though I spent some time
Searching for Jesus on the outside
No one came closer to Grampa
He was my Jesus on the inside.

That man gave me my pride
Always with him I'd confide
He was a hard-working man
The only one justified.

His smile was bright
His heart was light like a kite
He only wanted unity
Couldn't stand to see anyone fight.

He was always in the right
Helped me sleep through the night
Knowing I could count on him
Was my only delight.

HF

Growing up was full of feelings
Adults talked to kids so curt
My sister and I developed a secret code
To make sure no one's feelings got hurt.

If ever either one of us were saying
Anything unintentionally offensive in tone
We would always say to each other "hf"
And the speaker's voice would take a turn.

We'd clean up anything hurtful
As hf stood for hurt feelings
We made cards for new comers at school
Made sure they felt the healing.

No one had to tell me
I should develop this code
I wanted to be like Grampa
And that is how he rode.

I didn't have to imagine Jesus
I grew up with the best
Grampa was my Jesus
I kept him close to my chest.

Later on, in this poem book
I'll tell you a little more
I'm hoping you keep an open mind
As I write to even the score.

Angels

My stepfather's aunt
Was a very religious kind
She never had children
But worked hard for her grind.

One day she gave us presents
That hung over the bed
They were angels with holy water
But my sister must have felt dead.

My aunt gave me the girl angel
And my sister got the boy
My stepfather said it wasn't fair
And got her an extra toy.

I wasn't the one
Who handed out the gifts
But I always got in trouble
For starting the entire rift.

Like when we were young
Mom gave us colors to tell us apart
She gave my sister blue and I was red
My sister took that to heart.

Why does she get the "girl color?"
"That's not fair"
My mom sighed a guilty sigh
And felt major despair.

My sister was never happy
And it brought the mood down
She became the star in her own movie
And I played the part of clown.

I always tried to bring cheer
And make everyone laugh
But they wanted to guilt me
Deep down I was their gaffe.

Brownies

Now, I must be fair and convey
When Daddy John was on his game
He was like a hero out of a movie
He put the rest to shame.

I remember one time
I ran for Class President
My sister went out for Treasurer
And my mom paid the rent.

Daddy John wasn't working
Had to clean up his record
But he would cook our favorite dinners
And he never would wreck it.

So, one day we called from school
On a payphone
"Do you know who you're talkin' to?"
"The President and Treasurer," Daddy had known.

We both won the titles
And I was so happy
My sister actually smiled
Inside I didn't feel scrappy.

We came home to fresh brownies
Baked by Daddy John
Everyone was proud
Even my tired young mom.

That was a day
I wish there more
It's hard to appreciate the good days
When you're expecting the other shoe to hit the floor.

Traded

In the eighth grade
We tested the waters
Walked home from school for lunch
When that was against orders.

Catholic and public-school kids
Had many storms
Public-school kids thought Catholics were special
Because we wore uniforms.

Catholics thought public-school kids were favored
Because they had Pavonia pool in the summer
Catholics couldn't go there
Told we didn't have the numbers.

So, one day we were walking
Broadway, of course
And these little kids started pulling up skirts
It started with little force.

We let them giggle
As they were young
But behind them was a gang
And they felt really stung.

They waited for me to react
To see what I'd do
The first day I did nothing
The second day too.

But the third day was different
The little stinker grabbed my chain
It was my boyfriend's at the time
And it had a cross and gold name plate.

Well, at this moment
I had to decide
Was I going to crumble?
Or was I going to attempt to fight?

I knew at that instant
If I didn't react it would never stop
So, I gained my strength
And ran after the mob.

I chased them to the projects
Where I wasn't supposed to go
And in doing so I gained respect
They gave me a nod to and fro.

Now, I tell you that lesson
Not to say I am burned
But to show you how it works
And how the ghetto has turned.

The next day my stepfather found out
The girl's father worked with him
He asked if he could return the jewelry
To avoid the system.

My stepfather said "of course"
And that's how we played it
No need to get the girl a record
And that's how we traded.

Your Spell

When we were little, we would "call for" people
It involved knocking on doors and ringing bells
"Can the girls come out to play?"
We'd run out like bats out of hell.

Our apartment always had to be clean
Cause notice of visitors was slim
No one called ahead
People would come by on a whim.

Joe Sammartino lived next door
His father was greatly admired
No one messed with big Sammo
Unless they wanted to see themselves fired.

Little Joe was very sweet
He was my very first kiss
He got mixed in with the wrong Mafia crew
Gotta try not to reminisce.

The point to make is just how many
Poor Jersey City kids lost their lives
I can go name after name
All the ones who couldn't survive.

Not one counselor in my life
Has ever helped to ease my pain
Knowing how the Mafia had little choice
Needed money in the rain.

Not everyone could work white-collar jobs
Some folks felt too insecure
Using their hands was their thing
But blue-collar jobs were becoming obscure.

The only thing that helped me grieve
Was the song "Just a Moment" [34] by Nas
I'd often couple it with his "One Mic"[35]
Fight the demons in the garage.

My left hand would dribble so fast to the beat
I'd feel rage like I was Latrell Sprewell[36]
How many poor young Italian men?
Do you need to satisfy your spell?

Go straight to hell!

---

[34] Jones, N., Peacock, C., Rodgers, N., Edwards, B. (2004) Just a Moment [Recorded by Nas]. On *Street's Disciple* [Album]. L.E.S.

[35] Jones, N., Thompson, C. (2002) One Mic [Recorded by Nas]. On *Stillmatic* [Album]. Columbia, Ill Will.

[36] Onion, A., Sullivan, M., Mullem, M., & Zapata, C. (Eds.). (2009, November 16). NBA suspends Latrell Sprewell for attacking coach. History.com. https://www.history.com/this-day-in-history/nba-suspends-latrell-sprewell-for-attacking-coach

Bitin'

We used to hang out on the stoop
When it was late at night
My friend's big brother would crack on everyone
But I held my composure real tight.

"Nice pants you got there"
Was an everyday statement
I would never acknowledge anyone
Kept myself cool like the pavement.

I had one pair of black Lee jeans
And I wore them very well
Got them at Lord's on "the square"
Put the kids under my spell.

We used to talk a lot about "bitin'"
"Who bit off whom?"
Taking someone's style without crediting them
Would lead your butt to some doom.

Our Black friends used to say
Hip Hop bit off Italians with all the Mafia talk
We'd come to the rescue
Say we're all brothers and go on a walk.

Talking tough was our thing
When outsiders would try to sting
They'd pass us on by
Afraid to fight in our ring.

We had a lot in common
But the outside wouldn't know
Like when nosy academics came in
With their thoughtless radio show.

I'll write about that later on
For now, I'd just like you to see
Marion was a place like no other
We lived under the iron of the Pulaski.

Rosie Jane's

In the summers at night
We had Rosie Jane's
It was an Italian ice stand
We'd go even if it rained.

We'd sit outside
And talk a bunch of smack
I didn't do any drugs
But drank behind the train tracks.

It was one way we celebrated
Our ghetto life in the hood
It was one way we got together
And made our bad memories good.

Everyone dealt with something
Drugs were pretty big
Our parents tried climbing the ladder
But got shot down by a rig.

They brought drugs in to destroy us
What little fun we had
They couldn't stand to see us laughing
Cause their souls were that bad.

We were happy when poor
But the quest for more won out
The community broke apart
And all my dreams went to doubt.

I couldn't understand
Why families started to leave us
We had a real tight-knit community
But I guess they started to "skeeve" us.

Some moved to Nutley
Others moved to Bayonne
I couldn't understand
What they found missing at home.

But later on, I understood
The memories can get to you
The streets come alive
And you can feel traumatic residue.

But what those who left us behind didn't know
Was that sentimental ties to place are hard to break[37]
Though their suburban lives might have seemed better
Jersey City is an ethos no one can ever shake.

---

[37] Firey, Walter. 1945. Sentiment and Symbolism as Ecological Variables." *American Sociological Review. 10,* 140-48.

Volleyball

I used to be really good at volleyball
Daddy John always came to our games
We weren't living with him at the time
But he'd show up just the same.

He wore a long gray trench coat
And some thought he was odd
But when he showed up to my games
I'd say a prayer thanking God.

He'd come in as a spectator
Though he was good at every sport
He'd call the balls in or out
And I'd chase them all over the court.

Often, I'd serve the whole first game
Without anyone returning my serve
I'd get written up in the newspaper
Another shut out with J Bryan on the curve.

Outwardly, I was happy
I could do good with my hands
But inside I always felt conflicted
What about my sister's command?

I could never enjoy any achievement
It always had to be hushed
I didn't want to outshine anyone
So, I hid my feelings as I blushed.

Cheerleading

The coach called on the phone
And this is what happened
She said I made the team
Offered me position of captain.

"But don't get too excited
Your sister didn't make the team"
With those last few words
She crushed my entire dream.

My sister was right next to me
At the time we shared a bed
She started crying instantly
And inside I felt dead.

The next day I told the lady
I didn't want to join
Though I loved flips and cartwheels
With my sister sad I couldn't enjoy.

Three's Company

One day when we were little
Someone got toothpaste on the dresser
My stepfather pulled out a square water-pick box
And said it could tell the lying confessor.

I didn't do it
And I said just so
But he believed my sister
And punished me with a low blow.

That night I had to lay in bed
In the next room and listen
As they watched "Three's Company"[38]
Laughing and giggling.

Personally, I'd a said
"No thanks, but I'm tired tonight"
But they were out to get me
Angry and in a fist fight.

So, I sat for many years
With all the sick unfairness
My mom did similar things
Blamed me for them, careless.

One time I remember praying hard
For any kind of video recording
To tape all that they did
Without logic or any warning.

I know my sister needed to be favored
Because I was very popular with the kids
In eighth grade I was voted
Most athletic, all-American, and prettiest.

---

[38] Ross, M., West, B., Nicholl, D., Grossman, B., & Burditt, G. (Executive Producers). (1977-1984). *Three's Company* [TV series]. ABC.

I know that caused some hurt feelings
And my family called me a ham
Said I outshined my sister
Drowned me with guilt like a dam.

I just wanted someone to see
The unfairness and such
I wanted someone to rescue me
Out from under their clutch.

They always ganged up on me
And brought me all the way down
They wanted me disabled
So, they could steal my crown.

Like "Million Dollar Baby"[39]
They counted on the money
How much could we get?
From Gerber insurance, honey?

Maybe one day they'll realize
How loyal I once was
If I hit the number today
I'd still leave them my scrubs.

---

[39] Eastwood, C. (Director). (2004). *Million Dollar Baby* [Film]. Warner Bros. Pictures.

Filthy

That "free love" stuff of the 80s
Caused me a tremendous amount of stress
I wanted to preserve my modesty
But people didn't recognize the test.

I danced right along to Madonna[40]
Even though I recognized the lyrics
Were a bit too risky for a Catholic girl
Still, I had no one to play interference.

Someone viewed pornography[41]
And left many traces around
Used to have a book, *The Joy of Sex*
I would hide it when my friends came to town.

I developed really young
Fully grown by age 13
People would make comments
And I'd feel flush from the scene.

Even when I got older
Guys with their pick-up lines
"You look like a Victoria Secret model"
And I'd feel a chill in my spine.

But never would I let it show
The embarrassment there
I'd keep it all inside
Body objectified along with my hair.

I'd pretend I was too cool
And nothing bothered me
They saw me as someone fun
Inside I felt filthy.

---

[40] Kelly, T. & Steinberg, B. (1984) Like a Virgin [Recorded by Madonna] On *Like a Virgin*. Sire, Warner Bros.

[41] For one perspective on how pornography degrades women, please see MacKinnon, C. A. (1993). *Only Words*. Harvard University Press.

Heart Bleeds

I understand some had childhoods that were embarrassing
And some were treated bad for their skin
As for me, I lived in a house with mental illness
And my worst enemies were my kin.

I was about 16
When my mom ran away
Thought my stepfather was trying to kill her
Cause she outwore her stay.

We looked for three whole days
And nowhere could we find her
Then she called our Aunt Jay
And said "only tell Jennifer."

I went to the hotel
And my heart sunk to zero
My mom was barricaded in a bathroom
A thousand towels blocked as her hero.

Ma, what are you doing?
What is wrong?
Take me to the court
I have to sue Daddy John.

She had become a paralegal
And something got in her head
She saw his shady ways with money
And felt he was wanting her dead.

So, I fulfilled my promise
But my sister came along
She called home to warn him
Then in walks Daddy John.

My mother lost her footing
She couldn't hold her voice together
The bailiff was a neighbor
And I just wished for better weather.

The Judge ordered her for treatment
And they took her to a holding cell
I could see her smoking like a chimney
It must have been hell.

I vowed to try to help her
But she always blamed me
She said I broke my promise
And that's why my heart bleeds.

Cookies

In the 1980s crime was rising
No doubt from the drugs
But it was also from politicians
Wanting to see us fight like thugs.

Programs for the poor
Came with a lot of scorn
If you applied for food stamps
Inside you'd feel really torn.[42]

Everyone felt less than
We lived in the city
We knew from "Dallas"[43] and "Dynasty"[44]
Our lives weren't that pretty.

And then they started cracking down
On the Bonanno crime family[45]
Came in with wiretapping
Made it all real scary.

Then there were the kidnappers
We had to watch for their anger
Teachers said to come up with a code word
In case we sense any danger.

We came up with "cookies"
That was our word
If anyone was trying to take us
We'd make sure it was heard.

---

[42] Pruitt, L. R. (2016). Welfare queens and white trash. *Southern California Interdisciplinary Law Journal,*, 25, 289.

[43] Capice, P., Rich, L., Katzman, L., Hagman, L., & Horton, K. (Executive Producers) (1978-1991). *Dallas* [TV series]. CBS.

[44] Spelling, A., Cramer, D.S., Shapiro, R., & Shapiro, E. (Executive Producers) (1981-1989). *Dynasty* [TV series]. ABC.

[45] Talese, G. (1992). *Honor Thy Father*. Random House New York.

Then one day my mom called
From a pay phone in a mental ward
Screamed "Jennifer, Jennifer, cookies"
Asked me to bring in a sword.

I wanted to help her
But I just left her there like a punk
She was fighting off the demons
While my heart and soul sunk.

Tight

I was always expendable
My family had my twin sister
She was named by my mom
Reasoned the sick twister.

My mom was only 19
When she got pregnant
Physical attraction came to life
But I wasn't a planned segment.

I met Gary
At around the age of twelve
It was not how I wanted it to happen
But my mom wasn't herself.

I wanted him to be the one to reach out
But my mom tracked him to his phone, ah
I thought he would apologize
But he just blamed my nonna.

I suppose for him he tried
Bought us tickets to California
The first time on a plane
Was cool though I was torn, ah.

Daddy John knew we were going
And I felt really bad
Mom started to get back with Gary
And inside I felt sad.

Gary was a bit funny
Sarcastic and such
He didn't own up to any mistakes
Leaving us without much.

I was told he had money
But never cared to share
Gambled it all on horses
To recapture his snare.

He was in good shape
People remarked on his body
Mom wanted us to move to California
Go to high school for free was the lobby.

When Nonna found out
She literally choked my mom
"You're not taking these girls nowhere"
She was anything but calm.

When an Italian takes her right hand
And crunches it into a fist
Places that fist in her mouth
And bites down hard to her wrist?!

Man, you better move yourself out of her way
For, you have no idea what she's about to do
She'll lift you from a stationary position
Throw you forty blocks south on cue.

Thank God, my mom listened
I would have missed my friends
Especially Grampa
My heart would never mend.

But man, my mom was silly
Always looking for a dude with some money
She once dated someone 20-years older
Just because he had honey.

He had "connections"
And got her a court-house job
But we just missed Daddy John
Even if he was a working-class slob.

I credit my sister
For getting rid of that man
She tortured him to Heaven
He didn't fit the plan.

Nonna was also deeply embarrassed
She knew the man's ex-wife
Nonna told my mother
To get herself a new life.

Ultimately, she got back with Daddy John
And all seemed alright
Until the bills started overflowing
And our pockets got tight.

High School Tuition

One day at Saint Al's Academy
The Principal called me in
I wondered what went wrong
I tried hard not to sin.

She gave me a shot to my gut
Your tuition hasn't been paid
She said I'd have to leave the school
And inside I was afraid.

Gary had made a deal
To pay my high school tuition
It was supposed to make up for
Leaving us in so much friction.

I called him later that day
And asked what was going on
He said he heard my stepfather was back
So, get the money from Daddy John.

I was sick to my stomach
That I ever trusted his word
But I couldn't tell my parents
They'd only fight and feel hurt.

So, I decided to get a job
I started at age 15
I worked at "Vinnie's Pizzeria"
35 hours per week for the team.

Everyone at Vinnie's
Was like extended family
Egyptian Muslims taught me
All about the spiritual enemy.

I didn't mind working
In fact, I loved keeping busy
I still got near straight As
And paid the old bitty.

I still played volleyball
Still had time with friends
Now, I just had a little coin
I was happy and on the mend.

The Aeneid

In high school I was friends with everyone
But most of my classes were with Filipinos
I came to admire their studious ways
And tried adopting their religious ethos.

They were a very tight-knit group like Italians
But I already had my "in"
In my apartment building were Chris and Andrew
From grammar school I had my close friend, Trin.

In Latin class we worked really hard
Sister Helen Jean did not play
She taught us how to translate
And I even won her praise.

I once translated during class
It was a scene from "The Aeneid"[46]
When the father had to bury his son
Before his own life depleted.

I remember being sad
And thinking about this on 911
To see so many families
Lose their children to some Heaven.

Then it happened to my grampa
He had to bury his son
But like *The Revenent*[47] I went after them
And found the lonely one.

---

[46] Virgil. (2004). *The Aeneid*. Collector's Library.
[47] Iñárritu, A.G. (Director).(2015). *The Revanant* [Film]. 20th Century Fox.

Sore Thumbs

Working at the pizzeria
Allowed me to buy a dress for the prom
But I didn't have "the right" jewelry
And I couldn't ask mom.

That's when a friend
Came in with her plan
You can just shoplift
They won't throw you in the can.

I was confused
Catholic and all
But I decided to go with her
On a trip to the mall.

We walked into an accessory store
But I had no scratch
There were hanging rhinestone earrings
And bracelets to match.

My friend said "which one you like?"
And threw it all in her bag
It was more than $60 of jewelry
So easy for her to snag.

Part of me felt happy
I could wear those at the event
But another part felt slimy
They weren't Heaven-sent.

I had some other jewelry
Why didn't I just wear that?
Peer pressure set in
And I became a shoplifting rat.

I used to steal trendy clothing
That I couldn't afford
A few friends would do it together
And never were we bored.

But one day we got caught
When we went outside like bums
Perused a wealthier mall
We stood out like sore thumbs.

Trance

They used to call me violent
Said I kicked my sister out of the womb
They blamed a little infant
And brought her to a life of doom.

They accused me of giving her bloody noses
Each and every night
I had no idea what they were talking about
But I didn't put up a fight.

Then when we got older
I did begin throwing things out of anger
Frustrated by their lack of loyalty
They treated me like a stranger.

One day my sister was on the phone
And I had to go to work
She was supposed to drive me
But wouldn't get off with the engaged jerk.

I got so angry at her breaking sister code
That I got a can of Rave hair spray
I meant to hit the wall above her
But instead, it took her birth mark away.

She told me I attacked her identity
My family gave me the disapproving glance
Thank God, her birth mark grew back
I just wanted to break her from his trance.

The Prom

I was age 17
About to go to the prom
I pretended I was all together
But inside I was dying about mom.

The guys were coming to the block
In a freshly rented limousine
But my mom was going through
One of her famous mysteries.

She stayed inside the apartment
As she couldn't bring herself to walk
But she tried to crawl to the window
To wave to us with her big stalk.

The whole time I stayed praying
She wouldn't make the window sill
How could I explain
Why my mother looked so ill?

To my young outward self
I was happy she couldn't make the climb
We waved good bye to the block
But in my heart, I felt like slime.

How could I carry on?
And have a good time?
The only way I could do it
Was to block it out of my mind.

I became another person
Or personality to be more precise
This one was fun loving
Dancing for the prize.

But underneath were my lies
Inside I felt despised
My mother was losing her grip
Just like the man prophesized.

High School Graduation

High school graduation
Was a very big deal
I graduated with honors
And wore a blue ribbon for appeal.

My grandparents were all present
With buttons popping off their chests
But someone important was missing
My mom was in a hospital vest.

We begged them to let her out
Just to see the ceremony
But they said it would be a risk
And left her there so lonely.

When I visited her afterwards
She asked me how it felt
She never got to walk at her graduation
A race war caused her welt.

She was stuck in the eye with a pick
And her Black friends came to her rescue
But there were too many others that hated her
They told her to finish home school.

So, she never had a ceremony
Never got a real diploma
She went to school at Dickinson
It nearly put her in a coma.

Friendship

One thing that helped
When I was in high school
Was working at the Pizzeria
My friends were really cool.

I worked really hard
But it was all in good fun
I was the counter girl
Put the food in the oven.

I would take the orders
And I would ring in the prices
Mohamed made the pizza
And I would cut them into slices.

They called me "Ishta"
For the sweet cream on top
They said I was kind to everyone
Especially little Roberto who ran the mop.

One day Treach[48] came in
And autographed a small receipt
I put it in my lock box
And saved it so sweet.

Everyone was family
We'd laugh at each other
But they also suspected
Something was wrong with my mother.

Mohamed once talked to her
For a whole two hours
She'd call in the morning
And he'd practice his powers.

---

[48] Brown, V., Criss, A., Gist, K., & Rooney, H. (1991) O.P.P. [Recorded by Naughty by Nature] On *Naughty by Nature* [Album]. Tommy Boy.

It was embarrassing for me
But what could I do?
My mom was just in need of
True friendship too.

The Sting

It's a certain kind of feeling
When you visit your mom at the "spa"
She wasn't allowed her dove soap
She wasn't allowed even her bra.

Branded as a risk
Because her spirit was too great
Labeled bipolar
By a sick twist of fate.

Pumped with tons of medicine
To get that spirit down
She once looked for her eyes
In a suitcase while doctors frowned.

And then they almost sent her
To a state hospital
The lump in my throat almost choked me out
I felt her inner hostile.

But such is what happens
When you're a certain kind of mom
You're treated as someone envied
When really you feel alarm.

Everyone gangs up on you
And makes you fall from grace
They trip your feet before you
They make you lose that race.

But you look at her 18-year-old shot
And say "oh, see what privilege she has"
You'd never know the deep pain inside
You'd never know the sting behind her sass.

And now that she's been disabled
People laugh at her display
She cannot walk or work, my friends
She just sits in a chair all day.

Little People

Aunt Mary passed when we were in high school
That was Nonna's fun-loving sister
Uncle Alex and Uncle Danny came up from Florida
To pay their respects, plus they really missed her.

Our uncles stayed with us
Their long legs hung over our twin beds
We slept upstairs with Carmella
Her husband just passed and she was upset.

Uncle Alex constantly asked "where's the coffee?"
And he visited with his friend, "Beer Barrel"
I made him Veal Marsala
And he bragged about it to our cousin Carol.

He and Uncle Danny fought though
Usually over his smoking
"You're not my brudda no more"
Was often uttered in their 70-year-old argue-joking.

Still, I loved both uncles
Both were well over six-feet tall
Though Piccirilli means "little people"
Our Italian men would rarely fall.

Uncle Mark was one of the funniest
He would tell jokes all day long
He and cousin Nicky used to call up restaurants
Sent food to addresses all wrong.

I know it may sound immature
But that's the kind of humor they had
Lightened the heaviness of poverty
And made them feel good while being bad.

But make no mistake about it
As funny as he was
Uncle Mark wasn't one to play with
Just ask my little cuz.

One day my sister cut her hand
By carrying a mayonnaise jar
Uncle Mark showed up at the hospital
Because he knew they would try to spar.

Hospitals in Jersey City didn't like Italians
They thought of us as low white trash
But Uncle Mark pulled a doozy on them
He gave the doctor a run for his stash.

"Either you start workin' on her, or
I'll start workin' on you"
And just like that the doctor stitched her up
But it took Uncle Mark to come through.

Foxes

One Easter night "Foxes" had a teen night
And I was excited to go
Put on a new pair of ripped jean shorts
And a small pink sweater to show.

I met a cute boy that Sunday
He asked me for a date
He was from Country Village
I wasn't sure if Marion would rate.

But he picked me up from the Hudson Mall
Attempted to drive with me back home
When my friend's brother saw us on Broadway
He nearly kicked us off the road.

"I should slap your face" he said to me
It was for being seen with someone from another section
In Jersey City there were turf wars
It was supposedly for our protection.

I could more easily date an African American
Who lived within the Italian side of Marion
Than an Italian from the wealthier Country Village
There were so many rules to carry on.

There was Ege, Downtown, and the Heights
Journal Square and MLK
Marion was down below
And one couldn't walk astray.

But you all look to city life
Think the fighting is about Black and white
Never knowing that whites kill each other
Much more often than they act polite.

The Bluff

In the summer we had one air conditioner
And it stayed in my parents' room
There was a sheet to block the entrance
If we ever touched that sheet, we were doomed.

But every once in a while
We got to escape being poor
We got to feel the fresh cold air
While laying on their bedroom floor.

They'd put on "Charlie's Angels"[49]
And I loved Cheryl Ladd
I wanted to be a lady detective
And get rid of all the bad.

The bad were not Black folks
Not in this show
The bad were usually white
And that's important to know.

I also watched "Lady Blue"[50]
On the playground I'd practice my skills
Look for the one actin' up
Make sure that he was grilled.

I wanted to be a police officer
Then a detective
Ultimately an FBI agent
Until I went to college and realized whom they selected.

I didn't want to chase Black people
I felt they had been through enough
So, I changed my professional aspirations
And gave my heart to the bluff.

---

[49] Spelling, A. & Goldberg, L. (Executive Producers). (1976-1981). *Charlie's Angels* [TV series]. ABC.
[50] Gerber, D. (Executive Producer) (1985-1986). *Lady Blue* [TV series]. ABC.

In the Sun

Child abuse
It comes in many forms
But we still look to history
To try to correct the wrongs.

You want to avenge history?
May I suggest a way how?
Look to your own family
And watch as they take a bow.

Look at all the phonies
Take a good look at your nieces
Are they really happy?
Or dying into pieces?

What about Uncle Charlie?
Did anyone check on him?
Well, he was in good hands
I have to update my SIM!

It's a form of child-rearing
What got handed down
As a way to put people in their place
Lest one ends up with the crown.

Investigate your own family
And save this little one
The abuse you see as history
Still happens in the sun.

His Dish

When I was little
My stepfather made me eat soap
It was because I said a curse word
He tried to play me out as dope.

But I told him I liked it
Defiant I was
I asked how a little kid learned a curse
Then he shot his stinger in with a buzz.

Are you talking back to me?
No, never that
But have you heard the words used?
Or is your eardrum that fat?

I wanted to argue
But I had to hush
As punishment I had to scrub the bathtub
With a tooth brush.

It was an old bear claw tub
Porcelain in disarray
The black spots wouldn't come off
They were eroded away.

But I had to keep scrubbing
While they all laughed and ish
Young in the head
I had to deal with his dish.

They valued the Ten Commandments
And preached to honor your parents
There was nothing in those 10 rules
Protecting children from their rants.

So, later on in life
God gave me the updated Commandments
But when I sent them to my professor
I almost got sandwiched.

Uncle Mark

Uncle Mark always knew
When something was wrong
He'd pick us up and go sledding
I'd always feel I belonged.

He would also come by
With one of his girlfriends
They'd take us to the pool
And it eased the stress.

Uncle Mark served in Vietnam
And he was a very charismatic man
He had a heart of gold
Even if he didn't always plan.

He was one of my idols
And remains close in my heart
Archery was his game
He was very precise with his dart.

He walked around singing "My Way"[51]
And man, did he sing it well
Women flocked from all over to see him
He was good looking as hell.

Uncle Mark loved Eddie Murphy
He was not judgmental but had much humor
He was the life of every party
Could make you forget you had a tumor.

When Daddy John came back
Uncle Mark wasn't sure
But Nonna said forgive
As he was being tested by "the floor."

---

[51] Anka, P. (1968). My Way [Recorded by F. Sinatra] On *My Way* [Album]. Reprise

She felt bad for Daddy John because
His mother left at a young age
Grandpa Stanley met her at war in Germany
And freed her from that cage.

But something went wrong
Back in the states
She left Daddy John when he was little
And that formed part of his rage.

As long as it wasn't alcohol
Nonna could deal
Nonna's father drank homemade wine
Until he couldn't feel.

Nonna got stuck on anti-alcohol
Grampa could not have one beer
She never picked up a bottle
But still died of cirrhosis out of fear.

Point

His shoes were hard to fill
Impossible at best
How could anyone model him?
Better go get some rest.

He stood with excellent posture
His stomach extending beyond
Like a bear holding his hunted food
He waltzed in like a vagabond.

A welder by command
A fisherman by trade
He felt more than he let on
And never told if he was made.

Well, made men are now an afterthought
Does anyone recall the time?
We all protected our community's children
And it didn't cost us a dime.

But now we're told to hush it up
And let them walk all over the joint
Well, the wicked have over-crafted their stay
It's now time for the moral to point.

Enablers

You're an enabler
That's all I heard growing up in strain
Nonna went to "Overeaters Anonymous"
And they messed with her brain.

They never saw what food meant
To an Italian immigrant daughter
They never bothered to understand
How food helped mend the anti-Italian slaughter.[52]

They told her not to help my uncle
Because he was on "the sauce"
They told her to medicate her daughter
For acting like she was boss.

Like the hypocritical Christians
They believe in survival of the fittest
They won't help out a ghetto girl
They rather give her the grit test.

They get off on seeing her struggle
They pride themselves on making her wait
But she has a prayer about diverse loyalty
Just meet her at the gate.

---

[52] Cinotto, S. (2013). *The Italian American Table: Food, Family, and Community in New York City*. University of Illinois Press. See also Gambino, R. (2000). *Blood of My Blood: The Dilemma of the Italian-Americans* (No. 7). Guernica Editions.

Tigre's

Let me ask you a question
If you are allergic to cats?
But then take some Benadryl?
Will that calm the attack?

Well, yes it surely would
And that would be a help
But what if you lived with 14 cats?
Would that pill prevent your yelp?

No, it certainly wouldn't
You'd need your asthmatic inhaler
You'd need you a nebulizer
You'd need a Navy sailor.

For in no way would that allergy pill
Stop all the sneezing
The only thing it could do
Is slow down on the wheezing.

Apply that lesson to mental health
And this is what you get
Medication is only part of the answer
You need to be lifted out of debt.

You need people to cooperate
And not press on all your triggers
You need to be good to one another
Before you become one of Tigre's.

Maria

I grew up watching "The Cosby Show"[53]
That's how I learned about middle class
I wished my mom was like Miss Phylicia
I wished she had her smart sass.

I wished she made cool cupcakes
Like the other kids
But all she seemed to do
Was sleep and cry the skids.

If it weren't for kickball
And the fire hydrants in the summer
I doubt I would have made it through
My life was full of slumber.

But one thing I remember
That was really sweet
My mom would ripple the covers
And try to find our feet.

She would say "where's my babies?"
And we'd laugh and giggle
It didn't cost us anything
And our toes would wiggle.

There were also other things
Like once a year near Easter
We'd watch *The Sound of Music*[54]
She'd bake corn muffins for a feast, ah.

I loved Julie Andrews
And went around singing "Maria"[55]
My mom showed a softer side
It was rare but no one could beat her.

---

[53] Carsey, M., Werner, T., Kukoff, B., & Leahy, J. (Executive Producers) (1984-1992). *The Cosby Show* [TV series]. NBC.
[54] Wise, R. (Director). (1965). *The Sound of Music* [Film]. 20th Century Fox.
[55] Hammerstein II, O. (1959). Maria [Recorded by Nonbergy Abbey Nuns, the Sound of Music]. On *The Sound of Music* [Album]. RCA Victor.

Asthma

When I was six-months-old
My mom said I got real sick
She took me to the hospital
But the doctors sent me home with a stick.

They told her I'd be ok
But my mom knew something was wrong
She took a cab back to the hospital
And screamed until they heard her song.

I had real bad asthma
Possibly from the building
Also, my mom smoked while pregnant
Didn't realize it'd cause lung-killing.

It turned out I had a bad case of pneumonia
And I almost died
My mom refused to leave me alone
Didn't trust the nurses' side.

Hospitals at the time
Did not like poor Italian kids
They resented having to treat us
Rather see us live on the skids.

I've always been deathly afraid of hospitals
I used to get bronchitis and wheeze
Nonna would boil a pot of water with Vicks
Put a towel over my head so I could breathe.

She took me to the doctors
And made me some pastina
Minestrone soup for dinner
She was the best, my nonna Tina.

Rusty

One day on a Wednesday
When I was walking home from school
I looked out for Grampa's pumpkin car
But he was home fixing something cool.

It was a little drizzly
And I was a little sad
I thought I'd see Grampa
And he would remove the bad.

But at the corner of my eye
As I looked permanently down
I saw something shiny
And I didn't make a sound.

I picked it up quickly
It was an eight-link broken chain
It was silvery and dirty
But I picked it up just the same.

My uncle's dog was stolen
And the apartment wouldn't allow a pet
But I beat out the system
My new-found chain would hold the set.

I called that little chain, Rusty
And got me an old telephone box
I glued tissue paper to its insides
So, it was warm like a pair of socks.

I took Rusty to show and tell
And fed him baby food
I even had a marriage for him
We ate baked ziti as the coffee brewed.

That was one of my most cherished memories
But someone threw Rusty out
Thought he was a dirty little thing
And didn't have any clout.

But Rusty brought me years of happiness
He helped bring my family cheer
I found a way to take a piece of junk
And make him ghetto hero of the year.

The Feast

Every year on July 16th
Was the Our Lady of Mount Carmel Feast[56]
We looked forward to it all year long
Saved our money to buy some good eats.

They'd cook so much Italian food
The people would come from all over
It was one time of the year
We were proud of each other.

There were zeppoles, rides, and games
Even a wheel to win money
There were raffles, drinks, and desserts
Even struffoli balls of honey.

Extended cousins would come down
Pin a dollar on the Blessed Mother
Light a candle for their sins
Kneel before their brother.

It was a celebration
Like no other
Families from the projects
Also came through as our brothers.

---

[56] For a study of the importance of celebrating this feast day in Harlem, please see Zucchi, J. E. (1987). The Madonna of 115th Street: Faith and Community in Italian Harlem, 1880–1950 by Robert Anthony Orsi. *Canadian Review of American Studies, 18*(3), 446-447.

Damn Wranglers

I know some think we are flashy
When we walk a saint around town
But you wouldn't if you knew the real reason
That became a tradition of those held down.

Back in Southern Italy
The Gestapo would come in
Kill half of the young peasants
It was their way of keeping our numbers thin.

As an act of concession
They'd let us search for our fallen pillaged
If we were able to "sniff" them out
We could parade their bodies around the village.

We felt it was important
It was a ritual to free their broken spirits
They'd spit at us as we held a straight face
We internalized all our tears for interference.

Later on, when the Mafia was formed
They vowed to get them back
They went after the Gestapo
They made it a secret attack.

They killed in certain ways
Depending on the purpose
But they often cut up body parts in pieces
Believing it would spread out the evil surface.

The Mafia believed in reincarnation
And didn't want the evil spirit to come back in one body
They felt chopping it up into pieces
Would lessen the chance of them in the next life being spotted.

The Mafia learned to live looking over the shoulder
Never knowing when revenge would find its door
While this was about the Southern Italian "race"
It's also what happened to the world's most poor.

In addition to the Italian civil war[57]
The North decided to change the official language
Southern Italians had more than one hundred dialects
But had to bury them and learn to talk like strangers.

Damn Wranglers.

---

[57] Pavone, C. (2014). *A Civil War: A History of the Italian Resistance.* Verso Books.

The Raid

Don't worry about my psyche
Don't worry about my way
I can change personalities
Like Vickie Carpenter[58] in her day.

I can protect my inner heart
I can share my soul
I can make you feel my pain
I can make you long to console.

I am your inner conscience
I am your inner blade
I don't need your pejorative speech
I need you to start the raid.

---

[58] Quinlan, D., Stuart, J., Arley, J., Rauch, P., Gotlleib, L., Horgan, S., Levinson, M., Phelps, J., Tomlin, G., Valentini, F., Pepperman, J., Kwatinetz, J., & Frank, R. (Executive Producers). (1968-2013). *One Life to Live* [TV series]. ABC; The Online Network.

Lonely Song

Now look to cousin you know who
Some say he was a family man
But send some taboo booty his way
And he'll ruin their college plan.

Now he lost his children
And blew away all the money
Some things never change
Like hot tea and some honey.

But will they ever bow down?
And admit that they were wrong?
No, they'll die as martyrs
Singing a lonely song.

Karma's Hand

Look what happened to my loved one
Everyone thought she had it all
But when I needed a favor
She would never accept the call.

She traveled all over the world
To make a name for herself
All the while
Leaving two kids with no wealth.

When I was at my lowest
She was getting work done on her body
Left me to pick up my own pieces
So, she could show me up as shoddy.

I did not cause her downfall
It came from her own behavior
But you all can learn the lesson
Of never thinking you are savior.

For that was her problem
I take no comfort in her fall
But such is karma's hand
When you skip the monster's ball.

The Degradation Process

The degradation process is a slow one
It begins with the warmest embrace
Like a miraculous dream come true
To the humblest man of grace.

The degradation process is a slow one
It starts out nice and sweet
A card game and some comfort food
To thank him for his feat.

The degradation process is a slow one
Little by little jealousy seeps in
Soon his brand of raisin bread
Disappears like the digits on his vin.

The degradation process is a slow one
He can't drive a car!
Too old and feeble in the mind
Let me take care of his "bar."

The degradation process is a slow one
One day his bank account is wiped
Needed the money for *our* bills
Surely, he won't put up a fight.

The degradation process is a slow one
Soon he's all alone
His family left him in good hands
Said everyone but the throne.

The degradation process is a slow one
First Anne came to heal his infection
Got him to take a shower
By saying he needed to "pass inspection."

The degradation process is a slow one
Then he brings in Jean?!
Gets rid of the one who comforted him
To save two dollars an hour on a clean?!

The degradation process is a slow one
Jean he was no good
Sent from the State with all kinds of hate
He grabbed him as only he could.

The degradation process is a slow one
Jenny has gone mad
She's always worried about Grampa
Doesn't she know he's never sad?

The degradation process is a slow one
For those who cannot see
He pulls the wool over your eyes
As would the most wicked enemy.

The degradation process is a slow one.

Hell

Like a heat-seeking missile
They labeled me all along
Akin to Munchausen syndrome[59]
I became the ball in a game of ping pong.

Tossed back and forth
I was the scapegoat for all that went wrong
Even though I earned near straight As
They still sang a very sad song.

I thought if I excelled in sports
They'd see I wasn't sickly
Even though I earned many MVP trophies
They still saw me as rather sticky.

The doctors didn't help
Well, one day this could happen to Jenn
They taught my family to label
When I was in need of a friend.

The first time I went to a hospital
It was because of my dissertation
My family thought I was crazy
For trying to understand Islam and the Nation.

My professors at Yale didn't help
They could have come to plead my case
After all they were the ones
Who encouraged me to think beyond race.

Now, that it's all over
These harms of the past must be corrected
I understand times were different
But some of you definitely suspected.

---

[59] Schreier, H. A., & Libow, J. A. (1993). *Hurting for Love: Munchausen by Proxy Syndrome*. Guilford Press. See also Rosenberg, D. A. (1987). Web of deceit: A literature review of Munchausen syndrome by proxy. *Child Abuse & Neglect*, *11*(4), 547-563.

You could have stepped in to help
You could have reached out a hand
But instead, you withheld your invitations
And left me in cray-cray land.

I'm not complaining about it fully
For some humor did amount
But you left two young children
To live in a world of doubt.

You laughed at Charlene's clumsiness
You chuckled each time she fell
But you never cared to help her
That's why you're all going to hell.

Time After Time

He parked far from his destination
Never taking up top spot
"I could use the exercise"
Was his answer to his trot.

He never raced anyone to the finish line
He let them pass him on by
Better to stay slow and steady
Than sell his soul to modernity's sigh.

He walked up three flights of stairs
With grocery bags in each hand
If you tried to help him
He'd say he needed to balance his stand.

He never walked "empty handed"
He always carried his gifts
Took my pulse with his bare hands
With his touch my temperature wouldn't lift.

He wore clothing bought from Kmarts
And tinkered with his car
Never knowing I watched his every move
To me he was more precious than a star.

He was wiser than the three men
Who once guarded his stay
He wished only cheer to his family and friends
Though he mourned his son, My Way.

His funeral was attended by very few
He went out as a pauper
But the Navy played Taps[60] at the cemetery
As I felt "Time after Time" like Cyndi Lauper.[61]

I am his granddaughter.

---

[60] Taps, Arranged by General Daniel Butterfield, Union Army Brigadier General
[61] Lauper, C. & Hyman, R. (1984). Time After Time [Recorded Cyndi Lauper]. On *She's So Unusual* [Album], Epic Records.

Longing

I thought of you today
And the day before
I think of you everyday
Like the days when we were poor.

I remember the light of your face
And the moment you'd walk through that door
It was like Christmas morning
Just to see you one day more.

I'm thinking of the sacrifices you made
And all your artistic drawings
I wonder if you know you brought to life
Everything I could ever want in longing.

Now you're gone away
And I am still in mourning
Waiting for the day
I can stop myself from warning.

Unconditional love is what you taught
And you lived a humble life
I just wish I could have given more
Maybe one more game of cards or dice.

All you wanted to do
Was see your family smile
Friends of any background
Always welcome with no trial.

You were ahead of your time, Grampa
Someone who truly never judged
If only I walked in two minutes earlier
Would you have possibly budged?

Or would you have said
"Jenny, it's my time
God needs me up above
But I'm with you when you rhyme."

Christmas Tree

It's a day or two after Christmas
The presents lay a bare
The dinner is put away
The mom has tied her hair.

The children are exhausted
The parents feel much less
The entire uproar of Christmas
Has been a raging guess.

It hasn't brought you back
It hasn't cleared your name
It hasn't given us a direct path
To outwit the makers of this game.

It hasn't saved us money
It hasn't awarded a prize
It hasn't touched one tail of the devil
Seeping into lies.

But one day when the cover's removed
We'll remember who we can be
One day when our Muslim angels
Guard the true Christmas tree.

It will be a time for all
Conversion will not be the key
Acceptance will be the answer
And we will resolve all controversy.

The Seven Seas

The seven seas are restless
Sighing through the night
The party boat has left us
Fairies out of sight.

Where are all the loyals?
Have they now had enough?
Are they running for the valley?
Or have they mastered the bluff?

Wrong from Right

I hugged you when you were sad
I felt each tear you cried
If ever anyone called you a name
My insides would turn as you died.

You were my twin sister
I just wanted you to be happy
But you saw me as an enemy
Someone rough, someone scrappy.

No matter how many times
I tried to reach out to you
There was always something missing
Always something blue.

And now we're three years in
And I haven't heard your voice
I don't know if you realize
How much damage came from your choice.

I pray that you find a way
To make it back to life
Your children need to see you
You need to end this strife.

If the walls are closing in
I can provide the light
Just go back to when we were little
And remember wrong from right.

The Pale

The day I first visited Rutgers
Was a very happy day
I saw a whole new world
I couldn't wait to share my say.

I drove up to the block
And before I could even approach
I felt a pit in my stomach
An ambulance was on the road.

My mom had gotten out
And started running through the yards
Up and down the block
We had to chase her through the fog.

She got herself afraid again
And Nonna said we can't leave for school
We needed to stay and help with mom
Or else she would end up a fool.

That's when Daddy John stepped in
And found a way to make things up
"You go to college, Jenn
I'll take care of the sick pup."

So, he gave me my freedom
And man, did it kick in
I worked out like a champ
Got myself in good shape, fit not thin.

I earned near straight As in all my classes
And owe a lot to EOF's run
They paid for my college, room and board
Gave me an award at graduation.

I blasted Biggie[62] and Lauryn Hill[63]
I got real in tune with my gut
I lived life as I wanted
And got myself out of a deep rut.

The Ronald E. McNair Program taught me about a PhD
Dr. Grimmett gave me a fee waiver so I could apply to Yale
I owed her my entire life
An African American woman showed me how to beat the pale.

She paid for my first trip to present an academic paper
I felt like a million bucks
She paid then for a second trip
I felt like she brought me some luck.

And later on, when I had trouble
Dr. Grimmett's the one who straightened me out
"Don't you let them run you out of their school!"
My African American angel came through in a drought.

---

[62] The Notorious B.I.G. (1997). *Life After Death* [Album]. Bad Boy; Arista
[63] Hill. L, (1998). *The Miseducation of Lauryn Hill* [Album]. Ruffhouse; Columbia

Rutgers

When I went to Rutgers
I was really proud
My parents came with me
And Grampa, the shroud.

The whole family chipped in
Settling us into the dorm
I got to meet a new roommate
And had friendships to form.

But something was wrong
As usually happened
Mom kept calling the phone
Warning about entrapment.

I didn't know what to say to my roommate
We shared the phone
But my mom wouldn't stop calling
I had to shut the ring tone.

Then I got a job at
The SAC convenience store
I worked there throughout college
And even closed the door.

I had a full life
Did well in my classes
Though I held my faith
I began missing masses.

Then I met up
With a radical professor
Ended up with publications
On things that I severed.

He wrote about flag burning
And I did all the research
I found all the hidden cases
In a national search.

I didn't know the articles[64]
Would come out like that
Got my name in the lime light
But also, on the list that attacks.

Branded as a radical
Though my family served in world wars
I got myself on the list
It was the start of some scars.

In addition to academics
I went out my fair share
I didn't stay in my race lane
And was subject to much stare.

I had posters of LL Cool Jay
And Antonio Sabato Jr
Ended up meeting lookalikes
And they couldn't have come any sooner.

I championed racial equity
Long before it was in vogue
Never knowing that one day
I'd be cast out as rogue.

---

[64] Welch, M., & Bryan, J. L. (1996). Flag desecration in American culture: Offenses against civil religion and a consecrated symbol of nationalism. *Crime, Law and Social Change, 26*(1), 77-93. See also Welch, M., & Bryan, J. L. (2000). Moral campaigns, authoritarian aesthetics, and escalation: An examination of flag desecration in the post-Eichman era. *Journal of Crime and Justice, 23*(1), 25-45. See also Welch, M., & Bryan, J. L. (1998). Reactions to flag desecration in American society: Exploring the contours of formal and informal social control. *American Journal of Criminal Justice, 22*(2), 151-168.

Race Relations

One day in class on race relations
The teacher gave us a dare
She said write down a time when you felt discrimination
We began writing but she had a bad snare.

After about 10 minutes
She told the class to break according to race
She told the white students to rip up their paper
Said whites can't be disgraced.

She tried to teach a lesson about oppression
And said only a white person can be the villain
Said anything done to a white person
Is not the same if a "minority" does the killing.

Everyone looked at her stunned
Why not pair us up into couples?
Get us to know more about one another?
Let us share our troubles?

Like Denzel Washington in the *Titans*[65]
Why not get us to form cross-cultural bonds?
It is because the teacher wanted to impress Black students
Make them feel like she was their coat of arms.

Well, my Black friends told me to "forget her"
She knew nothing about my past
Nowadays, you all glorify her teaching style
It's like you want racial tensions to last.

Time to fast.

---

[65] Yakin, B. (Director).(2000). *Remember the Titans* [Film]. Buena Vista Pictures.

Ivy League School

Grandpa Stanley died in 1996
A few months later I received a paper
It said Yale is interested in graduate students
Who may fall below a GRE grader.

McNair had helped me out so much
I just wanted to make Dr. Grimmett proud
Could I apply to an Ivy league school?
And let the program bear the clout?

I wrote my personal statement
I did it over winter break
It was about how to unite Black and white
Let us see through all the fake.

The Chair of the committee
Decided to give me a chance
Even though I was late with my application
Had to wait for a fee waiver for that dance.

Then in February of 1997 I met him
It was around the day of St. Valentine
He asked me who the competition was
I said CUNY, and my heart wasn't fine.

It was all I could do but say "yes"
Yes, I'll come to your school
Not only will I study hard
I'll make it up to you, true.

Years went by and what happened?
I had one too many falls
Tried explaining it to my mentor
But he ignored my calls.

And now we are way into it
And he is now gasping at straws
All our leaders do is start wars.

Yale

When I got into Yale for graduate school
I wanted my biological father to admit one thing
My family must have done something right
For Yale to bring me under its wing.

But when he found out I got into Yale
He made the most callous comment ever
"Glad the genes were good for something"
He took credit for changing the weather.

And after his cruel comment
Going to Yale never seemed the same
He found a way to take something beautiful
And make me feel ashamed.

I still went in and tried my best
But things never felt right
I was now on the other side of privilege
And I didn't know how to fight.

I took each and every theory
And applied it to poverty and disarray
I envisioned my professors and I
Waltzing in to save the day.

But they would just sit there calmly
And spit out all this knowledge
About how to eliminate poverty
Why wouldn't they want to stop it?!

I was told Yale was a "theory school"
And I best rid myself of working-class thoughts
Though they couldn't touch the writing I handed in
They still charged me for the loss.

So again, I was branded as a radical
When all I tried to do was understand
They saw me as a troublemaker
Someone "hot" who needed to be fanned.

Dapper Dan.

Jersey City Accent

A young girl stood before you
Enthusiasm in her eyes
She praised your every word
She covered all your lies.

But never did she realize
Her you truly despised
It was her Jersey City accent[66]
That made you push her to suicide.

For that accent may sound uneducated
We do not pronounce the er
We replace it with an a on the end
And celebrate at the bar.

We pride ourselves on not being formal
Italians and African Americans together
You could not stand her optimism
You decided to change the weather.

Well, let me introduce you to Heather
She can knit you a real nice sweater
She can write you an outstanding letter
Bet that might make you feel better.

---

[66] Coggshall, E. L. (2017). *Short-a in the Sixth Borough: A Sociophonetic Analysis of a Complex Phonological System in Jersey City* (Doctoral dissertation, New York University). See also Rakić, T., Steffens, M. C., & Mummendey, A. (2011). Blinded by the accent! The minor role of looks in ethnic categorization. *Journal of Personality and Social Psychology, 100*(1), 16. See also Eula, M. J. (1998). Language, time, and the formation of self. *Italian Americana, 16*(1), 64-86.

Oh We

I took a leave from Yale
Because I had to work
Also, a Yale professor hated me
Wanted to see me die as jerk.

They taught Social Movements
But only cared about dense organization
Well, I learned from Martin Oppenheimer[67]
He knew everything about devastation.

I wrote that a charismatic African American leader will emerge
And they snapped back with "not so easy"
Then we all watched Barack Obama appear
And he presented as anything but sleazy.

I left and began a job at Columbia
I thought about transferring from Yale
Only to find years later
That professor ended up at Columbia, on my trail.

More will come of that story
But suffice is to say that when I write
Miracles can surely happen
I can bring you into this fight.

I don't mind doing it
I have the gift of prophecy
But you all fell asleep waiting
For the one to rescue thee.

Looking for a he.
Oh we.

---

[67] Oppenheimer, M. (1989). *The Sit-in Movement of 1960.* Carlson Pub.

Respect

I can tell you what's wrong with the hood
Everyone is in search of respect[68]
Countless ethnographers have uncovered it
But more still come out to inspect.

I don't know why they can't act on it
Create jobs and communities that bring recognition
Why, that would put academics out of business!
They'd be barred from the competition!

So no, they'll keep doing their studies
Try to find out something new
Never would they try to solve it
That is just something they don't do.

It's frustration-aggression theory[69]
But some only want to look at structure[70]
Never knowing how we internalize rage
Worse than the Hulk with a coke-bottle puncture.[71]

I married and tamed a six-foot-five Italian-Ukranian
You think I'm afraid of your rhetorical mantra?
Better go listen to "My Way"[72]
Take the byway with Frank Sinatra.

If you really wanna solve ghetto problems
You need to help kids heal from break up and divorce
No matter how tough little children try to act
Deep inside that kind of hurt has much force.

---

[68] Bourgois, P. (2003). *In Search of Respect: Selling Crack in El Barrio* (No. 10). Cambridge University Press.
[69] Breuer, J., & Elson, M. (2017). *Frustration-Aggression Theory* (pp. 1-12). Wiley Blackwell.
[70] Akers, R. L. (2017). *Social Learning and Social Structure: A General Theory of Crime and Deviance*. Routledge.
[71] Lee, A. (Director). (2003). *Hulk* [Film]. Universal Pictures.
[72] Anka, P. (1969). My Way. [Recorded by Frank Sinatra] On *My Way* [Album], Reprise.

Moms that turn their kids against fathers
Fathers who don't step up to the plate
What the hell has this world turned into?
You've created a place full of hate!

Still, you'll keep on saying the nuclear family is the problem
And I understand it's not for everyone
But for ghetto children who look for their parents
It's as important as a ray of sun.

So, please be thoughtful when choosing a partner
Please think ahead of the children
You don't want them feeling less than
Without any elders to provide them wisdom.

Catechism.

Don't You Dare

Screamed the girl
It was a phrase she learned
It was a time or two at just months old
Her eyes pierced envisioning him burned.

What being would hurt a child?
Especially in such a way?
What being, indeed, exactly?
Could go so far astray?

Is there any way to come back?
From breaking Jesus's rule?
Of never violating children?
One who's grown in the womb?

I never felt comfortable
To talk about what my mom said happened
But when I heard Jay Z's song "Anything"[73]
He helped with all his rapping.

He said something to the effect of
Replacing his face with that of my real dad
It was exactly what I needed
To change that sick disgusted feeling, bad.

---

[73] Carter, S., & Bart, L. (2000). Anything [Recorded by Jay-Z] On *The Truth* [Album]. Roc-A-Fella, Def Jam.

Rap

Throughout graduate school at Yale
I'd print lyrics from DMX[74]
I almost handed them to my professors
I thought he was Tyrannosaurus Rex.

At night I'd listen mostly to Nas[75]
Because I found him very serious
Although I needed cheering up
I felt like maybe he was hearing us.

Hip hop made famous
Stories that were just like the Italian mob
Growing up with such ghetto experiences
Their rapping made me sob.

I once listened to "Slippin"[76]
32 times in a row
Cried my eyes out on the subway
Thinking of the day Grampa had to go.

My counselor told me I was crazy
For caring about a 94-year-old man's death
Another told me I was "histrionic"
A third, "angry" like I was on some meth.

I turned my tears to music
That's the only thing that got me through
"He Ain't Heavy"[77] had me balling
As I relived Grampa dying on cue.

---

[74] DMX (1998). *It's Dark and Hell is Hot* and *Flesh of My Flesh, Blood of my Blood* [Albums]. Def Jam, Ruff Ryders
[75] Nas (1996). *It was Written* [Album]. Columbia
[76] DMX (1998) Flesh of My Flesh, Blood of my Blood [Albums]. Def Jam, Ruff Ryders
[77] Russell, B., Scott, B., (1969) He Ain't Heavy, He's My Brother [Recorded by The Hollies] On *Hollies Sing Hollies* [Album]. Capitol.

My Table

It was the spring of 2005
I had just published a book chapter
Then my life took a sudden turn
And it wasn't a matter of factor.

They stopped picking up my garbage
Because I wore the hijab
My Peruvian-cousin-in-law got detained
A friend was gun-point robbed.

My Goddaughter was only a few years old
Slept on the couch for a whole six months
Waiting for her mother to return
From the extremely insensitive runts.

They smashed into my car
And my neighbors wouldn't be a witness
Called me a "Muslim-lover"
Didn't understand I was in a fit-test.

My mom was back in a mental hospital
Screaming at all the nurses
I devoted myself to work
Tried avoiding their daily curses.

My sister wanted me out of my apartment
I was in Grandpa Stanley's house
She wanted to purchase it out from under me
Her colors showed through like a louse.

After all that time and money?
Spent fixing up Spruce with Uncle Mark?
After taking care of Uncle Ziggy?
They plotted against me in the dark.

A year prior my boyfriend offered to buy it
But I wasn't sure if it would work
I didn't want to exclude my sister
Though that's exactly what she did—what a jerk!

My parents had run out of money
Mom said their refrigerator broke
I didn't have the money to help them
But told her she could take mine to hold.

That would have left me with no fridge
A point she clearly didn't think of
"Your fridge is too small to cover the spot in my linoleum"
I slammed the phone down to the rug.

I worked at a minority-owned company
Once wrote my boss a Hail Mary pass
When the "journalists" began hounding me
I wanted my boss to take them to class.

But he wasn't actually from the hood
So, he didn't understand my coded-plea
Then my mom picks up the phone
Starts calling my boss, saying I'm crazy.

Some women of color didn't like me
I was the only white worker
Used to shut down the place late at night
Never scared of Newark or any lurker.

Then the police came crashing in
When I wasn't home
Ended up on the no-fly list
Restricted on where I could roam.

To make matters even worse
My mom tells me I was violated
Made me envision myself as an infant
And wonder why no one retaliated.

I threw a mug on her kitchen floor
Asked "why didn't anyone kill him?"
They called the police on me
Tried to play me out like a slap from William.[78]

---

[78] Blackwelder, C. (2022, July 29). *Will smith addresses Oscars slap, apologizes to Chris Rock in new video*. ABC7 Los Angeles. https://abc7.com/will-smith-apology-chris-rock-slap-oscars-2022/12082207/

You should have heard her harsh voice
It was possessed, like that of the Exorcist[79]
What a thing to say to a daughter?
What a thing to bring into my existence?!

I called the accused right away
Asked if it was true
"It was nothing I wouldn't do with a dog"
Was his answer, and I was through.

That's when I first felt suicidal
That's when I felt as broke as someone homeless
To watch my twin sister so carefree
I crawled in a ball and became hopeless.

My family had decided I would be better off
Not working in the "real world"
They wanted me to collect disability and move in with them
They threw the kitchen sink at me, hurled.

I called my mentor in Connecticut
And begged him to call my stepfather
I sensed the heat from all directions
And wanted him to save his academic daughter.

Even though he is the expert
On what Sociologists call "labeling theory"
He never stepped in to stopped the process
I guess he just wasn't hearing me.

So, I ended up with a label
While my mentor sold my life as fable
The police marked me down as unstable
As Psychiatrists set my table.

A story fit for cable.

---

[79] Friedkin, W. (Director). (1973). *The Exorcist* [Film]. Warner Bros. Pictures.

Rocky III

My stepfather took me to my favorite movie
It will always be *Rocky III*[80]
The sad music when Mick died
Would soon become my destiny.

You want to know why he did cocaine?
I can answer it partially
His father was a "driver" in the war
And the people hounded him royally.

Daddy John had a broken heart
In part for what happened to his father
Though he doesn't talk about it
It's obvious the man had a stalker.

In 1995, Grandpa Stanley had a big fall
Aunt Blanche thought he was just drunk
Let him sleep on the cold bathroom floor
Tired of him drinking like a skunk.

The next day he went to Christ hospital
He seemed ok but talked a bit odd
"Jenn, there comes Shasha the cat"
From the top right wall like he was God.

He made eye contact with me many times
And I felt he was in danger
My young mind didn't process WWII
As the source of some folks' fierce anger.

They said he suffered massive strokes
And sent him to a special rehab
They put tons of plastic tubes on him
They treated him like a rat in a lab.

---

[80] Stallone, S. (Director). (1982). *Rocky III* [Film]. MGM/UA Entertainment.

When I visited he used to plea
"Jenn, get us a couple sodas"
My heart would break into a million pieces
They said he couldn't have any liquids, let alone Coca-Cola.

I knew something was not quite right
I could tell by the looks of the nurses
Someone was paying Grandpa back
For his role in helping to stop Nazi curses.

He stayed on tubes for more than one year
And Daddy John said "never again"
He tried to care for all our elderly
So, they wouldn't be tortured by "them."

Years later that same hospital
Down in Neptune, New Jersey
Named the street after Grandpa Stan
Bragged that they left him no mercy.

With a will opposite that of Nakam[81]
These secret groups invoke revenge on U.S. soldiers
Both my sweet and loving grandfathers
Were killed as if they were Whitey Bulger.

Well, I walked into that hospital
Several years after he died
I demanded to see Grandpa Stanley
They saw the look of death in my eye.

The security guard said "please behave"
The nurse gave a laughing little twitch
They knew I was the granddaughter
Of the one they let die in a ditch.

What a witch
But now I must switch
And tell you about all he risked
To wake me up from their drift.

---

[81] Porat, D. (2022). *Nakam: The Holocaust Survivors Who Sought Full-Scale Revenge.* Stanford University Press.

I went to the hospital on their shift
They stopped my breathing with their lift
Planned to steal me and leave everyone miffed
Until Grandpa Stanley appeared with his gift.

I woke up to angels carrying me
"We'll get you away from the meanies"
I was freezing cold inside
And they were my God-given genies.

They took me to another hospital
They said to stay alert
They said the man would come in
To stop me from being hurt.

I knew right there I had crossed over
I remember feeling "Heaven"
But I had my eyes wide shut
So, I wouldn't get scared by the Leven.

Then one day they brought him in
He was an old blue-eyed homeless man who didn't rate
The nurse sprayed Lysol all around him
While I felt in my heart it was fate.

I knew I could only ask one question
So, I asked what was his name
He looked me in the eye seriously
Said "Joe" and I knew he was fame.

The other patients were around him
And one reminded me of Mick
He told me to make my bed
And listen, so they wouldn't call me "sick."

He told me to write a letter
About how this was all unfair
I followed his lead religiously
Took the medicine to get the hell out of there.

Then I went to see another doctor
He said I had PTSD
But the people didn't like that label
They wanted me to fulfill my family tree.

My mom's doctor called the hospital
Without ever even seeing me as a patient
Said Jenn "has to be bipolar"
Just like her mom, man was he ancient.

The hospital went along with it
And no one came to my rescue
Except Grandpa Stanley in a homeless body
Warned me about the impending screw.

So, if you ever tell me I'm crazy
For caring about those who died
I'll stare you down to your skeleton
With the power of the one crucified.

My pride.

Like Mike

You think you know my weakness
You label me as you like
This when something bad happens
You can moonwalk it back like Mike.[82]

You say she can't be a victim
A victim of gaslighting[83]
Once you're labeled bipolar
Your word is as good as zodiac sighting.

You can be tortured at work
You can be followed home
No one will believe you
Not even the Pope in Rome.

Everything becomes your fault
Everyone believes the enemy
You can be killed for sport
And they'll say you caused it anyway.

What a day!

---

[82] Effron, L., & Welsh, S. (2018, May 23). *How Michael Jackson learned to 'moonwalk*. ABC News. https://abcnews.go.com/Entertainment/michael-jackson-learned-moonwalk/story?id=55336603
[83] Sweet, P. L. (2019). The sociology of gaslighting. *American Sociological Review, 84*(5), 851-875.

This Dance

I understand you feel unsteady
And not sure of your path
I understand you feel sorry
And fearful of God's wrath.

But might I suggest there is still a chance
You can make up for your bad deeds
All you have to do
Is be like the one who bleeds.

I sent you messages years ago
I selected you for the position
I know you're 44 some years my senior
But I have remarkable intuition.

Honor the Commandments I gave you
Not the ones they were from Musa
Humor me on some short stories
And take a visit to Port Saint Lucia.

Just make sure I am more than ok
And you'll find I can write you a movie
Show you all the do's and don'ts
Restore you to your beauty.

Make good on what went wrong
And you'll find your second chance
Ignore this message, however,
And you will lose this dance.

The Rhapsody

It's a quarter after midnight
And she forgot her rose
Placed it on the cobweb
While they watched it decompose.

The Banana spirit's with her
He fights with every breath
Knowing that mental illness
Was not the true cause of his death.

But somewhere beyond the rhapsody
This man has found his low
He screams out to the valley
"Your reign is all you know."

Then one day when the sugar snap peas
Form their very own base
You'll examine the true maker
Of this here human race.

The White Dove

Exhausted at the window
Waiting for a sign
The white dove hasn't come down
And neither has the wine.

The candle sticks are ready
I can hear them from the floor
They're asking if you feel them
Burning to the core.

I had to send you to the wolves
Your politics were erratic
I had to put you to the test
Needed to see you patriotic.

Now the days are falling away
And I can see you live like Joseph[84]
Kept in a well with all kinds of hell
Citing lyrical strings from K'Naan and Mos Def.[85]

Your loved one was so jealous
Some cousins, how they mock you
Yet, they've never been to Yale
Never met the cashew.

But you stay steady climbing
And I will do my part
I have never left you
Been here from the start.

So, if you ever wonder
Just where in the world is God?
Think of our conversations
Before they plot against your pod.

---

[84] Devine, E. M. (1997). The Coat of many colors: Service, education, and religious schools. *Religion & Education, 24*(1), 76-83.

[85] Smith, D., Warsame, K. (2007) "My God" [Recorded by K'Naan featuring Mos Def] On *The Dusty Foot on the Road*.

Revelations

Like a runner in a famous restaurant
She travels to and fro
She hoped you'd see her efforts
And back her up when it's time to go.

But all you ever seem to do
Is wait like a lazy man
Don't you know Revelations is a book?
It's there to help you plan.

An Alley

She saw him in an alley
And he slid down the rope
She only tried to reach him
But he was out of hope.

The world can be so cruel
And time is not always kind
You can play as hard as you like
But you cannot hit rewind.

The actions that make you
Will fill your words with doubt
Like the signs on a Jersey highway
You have only moments to choose a route.

So, when opportunity comes for you
I pray you'll never choose wrong
Life has a funny way of making you
Watch as your heart bobs along.

Guardians of the Lucky Pot

How many days spent wondering?
Why someone would do such harm?
As if children are worth nothing
Like throwaways on a farm.

How could they not remember?
That God he sends us signs?
Through our blessed children
Here to help us with our lines.

How could anyone cause destruction?
To what the Lord has made?
How could anyone feel repulsion?
Just because they are afraid?

Whitney begged you to consider your miracle[86]
And not to throw it away
My God, these are innocent babies!
Your ancestors coming back to help you play!

But you consider them "cells?"
And care only about physical pleasure
My goodness, you have no discipline!
You're weak beyond all measure!

You follow the evil who wish to get back at God
For making them as he did
Angry over what they wish they had
They try to shame God's way like a kid.

They try to lure him down
To deal with such a mess
To protect all of his children
From dealing with such stress.

---

[86] Reid, L.A. & Babyface (1991). Miracle [Recorded by Whitney Houston]. On *I'm Your Baby Tonight* [Album]. Arista.

But they know that God can't come down
Not right at this time
For he is busy fighting battles
Of which you do not wish to find.

And if he comes down to save
Each and every ham
We will be in a bigger mess
So, please remember the dam.

Now, if I can make a suggestion
It would be just one
Take care of what is troubling
Take care of your own son.

If your children act out of step
Remind them how to be
And remember where we all came from
Good ol' Galilee?

No, I mean the other motherland
The one in Italy
The message is from thereabouts
Rebuild your family.

The time is not to argue
The time is not to chill
The time is to protect our children
From crumbling at their will.

There's strangeness in the world today
Of very great magnitude
Like werewolves dancing in the street
On an episode of "Kalamazoo"[87]

So, answering your questions
About why this happened to you
Is like ignoring all the ways
It's still happening today too.

---

[87] Forcier, A. (Director). (1989). *Kalamazoo* [Film]. Les Ateliers du Cinéma Québécois

The reason is always the same
They wish revenge on God
If you see yourself as his child
Then use the carrot and the rod.

Don't let them hurt God's children
They belong to our lot
We are their protectors
Like guardians of the lucky pot.

Stockholm Syndrome

I'm sorry your family hurt you
I'm sorry they don't see your worth
I'm sorry for all the hospitals
It's been happening since your birth.

I know you find it difficult
To believe people could care so little
But you have Stockholm syndrome[88]
And they're as guilty as the fiddle.

I would say to get a few good people
And form a supportive click
Remember the good times from years ago
But also, how the bad ones made you sick.

And like your twisted loved one
The one who dragged you through the mud
They project their evil onto you
And then act like Elmer Fudd.[89]

So that when you wake up punch-face
They'll say it was something you did
This way they keep you under their thumb
And all three of them act like a kid.

Find a set of normal boundaries
And guard them with your life
The insanity of your family
Has been your biggest strife.

---

[88] Reid, J., Haskell, R., Dillahunt-Aspillaga, C., & Thor, J. (2013). Trauma bonding and interpersonal violence. In *Psychology of Trauma*.

[89] Schlesinger, L., Harman, H., & Ising, R. (Creators). (1930-present). *Looney Tunes*. Warner Bros.

Come True

It was the day of Good Friday
She knelt in the pew for hours
Watching the stations of the cross
Her butt never touched, their powers.

She felt a sudden tug
And her abdomen seemed to tighten
Were the angels sending a sign?
Or was someone there to frighten?

She felt the presence of Mother Mary
Asking her for a slight
She didn't know if she could hold it
The baby with all her might.

But she said to Mother Mary
"If you think I can help?"
"I will meet you years from now
Just hold on to your welp."

She held on for many years
But Grampa's time was near
She didn't have much left in her
And felt she couldn't steer.

But the seedling became an infant
And even passed onto a toddler
Now she's a big girl
And the woman, a raging monster.

You never know what God gives you
So be careful if you sense a trap
Take it to your writing
And the truth will always rap.

Then one day when you're sorry
And see all she's been through
Pick up where she left off
And make Revelations come true.

Waterfalls

"Don't go chasing waterfalls"[90]
I wish I had taken this advice
If I didn't climb that ladder
My family might still be playing dice.

But when you insult a mean man
By out-writing his every clause
It can make him angry
And wish to put you on pause.

For if those words could come alive
And reach out to the masses
There's no telling how many people
She'd influence in our classes.

Her paper on Marx,[91] Durkheim[92] and Weber[93]
Sent one asking for a promotion
But another read it differently
Said she's the one to cause commotion.

A radical liberal I was coined as
A far cry from my working-class roots
My family became full game
Gotta trick them out of their boots.

I'll start with her favorite uncle
Since he is an idol
I'll screw with him at work
Sit back and read her Bible.

---

[90] Etheridge, M., & Lopes, L., (1995). Waterfalls [Recorded by TLC] On *CrazySexyCool* [Album]. LaFace, Arista.
[91] Marx, K. (1986). *Karl Marx: A Reader*. Cambridge University Press.
[92] Durkheim, E. (1973). *Emile Durkheim on Morality and Society*. University of Chicago Press. See also Durkheim, E. (2005). *Suicide: A Study in Sociology*. Routledge.
[93] Weber, M. (1978). *Max Weber: Selections in Translation*. Cambridge University Press. See also Weber, M. (1993). *The Sociology of Religion*. Beacon Press.

This way they won't suspect me
I'm pristine in my planning
I'll blame it on Agent Orange[94]
Get them angry about the tanning.

But really it has been me
Behind it all the time
Even sent in Jean
To grab Grampa from behind.

Meanwhile at the household
He'll sit looking pretty
The father of morality
Deep down is one to pity.

But still his word can kill you
He'll wave as you extend your hand
He's out to avenge his people
While you're just trying to understand.

---

[94] Frumkin, H. (2003). Agent Orange and cancer: an overview for clinicians. *CA: A Cancer Journal for Clinicians*, 53(4), 245-255.

Crash and Burn

It was a very long time ago
When God selected Noah for the trip
His family was impeccable
And God gave Noah the clip.

He was to start an example
He was to make a new
He was to select two of a kind
And bring them on the ark, too.

Noah did all he supposed to do
But didn't truly get God's direction
The election of two
Was to warn of his rise to perfection.

Then God sent him the message
The coast is now quite clear
Get yourself out of the ark
And lead my people, so dear.

But Noah hesitated on the message
Preferring to stay big man on campus
He was King of his God-given ark
Playing God like a praying mantis.

God kept on sending him messages
Some in the form of a letter
But Noah kept his head in the sand
Thinking he knew better.

Waiting for Noah has become an eternity
For somewhere his heart grew too sad
He decided to play the role of God
And tried to get rid of the bad.

He noticed seeds of war
He noticed contenders afar
But when it came to American students
He felt we belonged on the tar.

For he too thought we were spoiled
And needed to learn how to save
He too thought we were lazy
And needed to work like a slave.

Some wanted to crush folks with hardship
Claiming it was to instill compassion
But for many on the receiving end
It felt worse than a deadly cast out of fashion.

I understand Noah's lesson
We certainly need to learn
But how many more sad lessons?
Until we crash and burn?

Lifeline

I cannot explain the joy I feel
When I hear your name
It's like meeting God for the very first time
Yet, he's exactly the same.

I searched for many years
Decades to be more precise
But I couldn't find your smile again
It was hiding behind your device.

I understand you trusted me
But I think I'm out of tricks
No one would ever believe me now
I've been hit over the head with some bricks.

How can I protect them?
When I have to work?
How can I smile at them?
When they try to twerk?

My will has been eroded
Some academics set me an evil maze
I thought I would just plant my seed
And hoped someone would graze.

I will do my best, of course
If it is God's will
But can you throw me a lifeline?
Some money instead of a pill?

Bought

I feel the heaviness in my heart
About what I discovered
A bitter man with bitter ways
Like a helicopter, always hovered.

I can feel the matrix in the air
Its smut is growing slowly
They came down and crowned the man
Because they thought him holy.

And so, he holds the power
He holds the forbidden key
He holds the power to end the world
Or bring us simplicity.

But he chose to drive us crazy
He chose to make us mad
He chose to sell my soul to the devil
And watched as they raided my pad.

The poem I wrote beyond anger
Is part of me that wants to forgive
But the part of me here right now
Does not wish this man to live.

And so, I pray for forgiveness
For having a very mean thought
I suppose it comes from going to Yale
And watching my life be bought.

Sold

Can I ask a favor, friends?
My will is fading fast
I haven't got much left in me
My life is in a cast.

I just want to be a mom right now
But life is getting in the way
It's pushing me to right a wrong
In order to live another day.

It moves around magically
And rarely announces itself
It appears when you least expect it
Like the mystery elf on the shelf.[95]

When you catch hold of what's inside
You won't be able to fold
You'll know that she has come to hold
The tragedy of being sold.

---

[95] Aebersold, C. V., & Bell, C. A. (2005). *The Elf on the Shelf: A Christmas Tradition.*

Mental Telepathy

What is Jesus to the Pope?
What is Jesus to a Pres?
What is Jesus to a Psychiatrist?
Nothing but a threat.[96]

The Indian women warned me
They circled around my block
But you would not know how
They sent me messages through the dock.

My research confidant was taken into custody
And my Peruvian cousin-in-law was held in jail
All because I was helping Muslims
They punished my loved ones with a tail.

But the streets came through with warnings
They told me you were planning to burn my house down
The homeless woman also told me
Not to make a sound.

I don't need your word, my friend
I know more than you can see
My gift comes from my grandparents
We call it mental telepathy.

---

[96] The beginning of this poem is inspired by Frederick Douglass. Please see Douglass, F. (2019). What to the Slave is the Fourth of July?. In *Ideals and Ideologies* (pp. 377-381). Routledge.

Hospital

I hath told you what to do
If the film, Gaslight,[97] brings you down
Take him to the hospital
And let him have a go round

Tell him he's acting violently
And subdue him as a pest
Treat him as a sickness
From which we're faced a test.

Lock him up with his family
Place them all in one room
See how long it takes
For one to kiss the broom.

See how long it takes
For one to turn on another
Like rats caught in a silver wheel
Trying to outdo their brother.

See how long it takes
Before his label sets in
Before he's in a padded room
Screaming "Evil, Dr. Chin!"

Then one day when no one's looking
Tell him you know what he's done
Tell him it's time for his karma
And ask if he finds it fun.

---

[97] Cukor, G. (Director).(1944). *Gaslight* [Film]. Metro-Goldwyn-Mayer.

Clairvoyance

You want to know my source of feeling
Because it cuts that deep
You rather ask my source of healing
Before it's your time to reap.

If my presence is an annoyance
Because it makes you think
Then my absence with be clairvoyance
When it comes your time to blink.

Boss

You can call me crazy
You can think you're sane
But when the reaper comes for you
You'll be looking for me in vain.

I am here to tell you
You need to pick up the belt
The grass is gaining on us
And looking to make a welt.

Organize yourselves together
But pretend you still have a rift
This way when they come for you
A friendly will pick up the drift.

And they won't know what hit them
They'll clamor at the loss
But one thing they can never do
Is claim that I ain't boss.

No One Cares

I'm sorry for all the writing
In a very deep way, I feel bad
I don't mean to hurt my loved ones
It's just my inner voice is sad.

I have crept into the basement
But I have also gone upstairs
It's not a place you want to go
You're an invalid and no one cares.

I'm Sorry

I took some time to heal
I took some time to grieve
Much of it was done in public
Which prompted many to leave.

It prompted many to snicker
It prompted many to laugh
It prompted many to judge my family
Diss my husband and my calf.

But the friends I have who've stayed
I will treasure you more than you know
And when I get my day with the Lord
I will make sure he sees your go.

The pain of healing trauma
Does not come in any one way
You fight with every ounce of courage
To make it through another day.

And to my lifelong husband
You've stuck with me thick and thin
You've been passed over by some friends
You've been cast out by some kin.

But what you've shown is power
Loyalty to be more precise
And in kind you will have your place
I only hope it can suffice.

For the folks who see you as Mr. Nice guy
Or a push over in your sleep
There will come a day they bow to you
When it comes their time to reap.

And on that day, you will be magnanimous
For you are God's best son
Far from the average hustle
Far from everyone.

So, raise your hand and care not
Who invites you to their party
Know in your heart you're better
They ain't worth their cheap "I'm sorry."

In a Crunch

She fell back into compliance
With a shell harder than steel
She cannot share her visions
Unsure if anyone can feel.

The fire-folks are ready
Steadfast in their hope
They've seen the devastation
They've climbed the tattered rope.

Where is all the foundry?
Have they all passed the flue?
Are they hiding in the valley?
Are they returning from the blue?

The mass is growing empty
The clan is growing strong
But some will never stand up
And admit that they were wrong.

How we startle silence
Is pass it down the punch
The glass remains half empty
But needed in a crunch.

Shunned Away

He saw her from a distance
And hid behind his phone
He knew he made a grave mistake
By judging her for her clone.

No one had ever been through
All that she'd been through
No one in the entire place
Had ever survived a coup.

Yet, they watch her every word
They laugh and snicker too
They have not good intentions
They haven't the slightest clue.

But somewhere deep inside
Where the cows can't graze
They know they've done wrong
And they begin to fear the blaze.

Should I bother saying hello?
Or should I take a chance?
I can pretend I didn't do those things
But will she always peep my dance?

Then one day when he's older
And faces his dying day
His life will flash before his eyes
And he'll see no other way.

He has to make it up to her
Lest God leaves him all alone to pray
He never thought he'd see her
The one the whole world shunned away.

Like a Kite

She receives butterflies in her arms
And then begins to write
It might seem like a daunting task
But she can channel like a kite.

It slows from her arms to her hands
And the messages begin to type
It takes roughly two minutes
For each poem to recite.

She does not begin with a topic
As that comes from the source
He's quiet as the midnight
And forceful without force.

She's often surprised by the written word
And hopes only that it works
The messenger is only a messenger
She needs you all where evil lurks.

Your Dove

When I think about you
And all your wild ways
I wonder if you'd ever known
How much I admired your plays.

You were my grandmother
Nonna to be more precise
When I scraped my knees
You'd kiss them with your life.

You cooked many a meal
When mom was in a way
You picked up every bad vibe
And tossed them all away.

You let me create a wall
Of pink construction paper J's
Even bought me a decorative umbrella
To make it through the rainy days.

I wonder if you know
How much I care for you
When you'd cry, I'd stop breathing
Try to cheer you out the blue.

Now that you've crossed over
I still see you now and again
Sometimes you're a woman shopping
Others my only friend.

I want you to know I love you
My nonna up above
Keep sending me your signals
And I'll keep a look out for your dove.

Grampa

My grampa was born in Baltimore
Original name was Buckie
Moved down to Virginia
Six brothers and sisters made him lucky.

He grew up making bread
And tending to the farm
He was friendly with African Americans
And never meant any harm.

He told me about the mood down south
And how it was so wrong
He told me to be "extra nice"
When anyone Black comes along.

He told me about the "n" word
But never did he utter it
He said if I hear it around town
Make sure to call it quits.

His grandfather's name was
Mack
He told Grampa he had a "sissy name"
And to change it before the attack.

Grampa admired his uncle Charlie
And so, he took on that name
His grandfather stood proud
Didn't want his pup being shamed.

But his mother died at a young age
And Grampa's father had to work
Then his grandma died
And the family got really hurt.

Grampa's father, Clarence
Said half the kids could travel up north
There was no work in Virginia
But he would travel back and forth.

Grampa, his brother Lenny, and two sisters
Went up to New York to stay
But Grampa got sick with pneumonia
And the State took the kids away.

So, Grampa grew up in an orphanage on Staten Island
His mother died at a young age
Seven brothers and sisters in all
Had to see his siblings through a cage.

He rarely talked about it
Except a kind word about the nuns
He converted to Catholicism
At the age of 18, they drafted him and gave him his guns.

One time in his loneliness
He told me something that hurt his climb
"All them years in the orphanage
My father came to visit me just one time."

Made fun of for his southern accent
He was teased throughout his early years
But he still stayed above the fray
And never cowed down to their fears.

He had a pretty fierce stutter
But an old Navy man knocked it out
Told him to stop and think about his words
Gave him confidence in the face of doubt.

He was the kindest man in the world
And man, if he called you friend
That would mean he would do anything for you
It wouldn't matter your race, gender, or political bend.

He was good-hearted at all times
He was a medic in Okinawa[98]
Some put him on a list for once
Healing an opposite warrior.

---

[98] Sloan, B. (2007). *The Ultimate Battle: Okinawa 1945--the Last Epic Struggle of World War II*. Simon and Schuster.

They used to haze him in the service
They knew he had a southern draw
They sent him into an all-Black barracks
Just to see if they could shake Grampa.

Grampa walked in with his instrument
Waking everyone up
Something about him was wholesome
And they didn't shake his cup.

The guards used to pack mashed potatoes
Heavily onto his plate
They told him he had to eat every bite
Or else he wouldn't graduate.

Grampa wasn't fazed at all
Mashed potatoes and gravy were his thing
He ate every last morsel
And the guards couldn't do anything.

One time they asked him to guard a man
Who was responsible for killing his friend
They wanted to check Grampa's morality
But he was Heaven-sent.

He held the boa with his right hand
And gave the Japanese man a good look
Why did you go and do that?
Inside the man must have been shook.

But Grampa would never hurt a fly
And that's what they wanted to see
George HW Bush was in the Navy at the same time
It must have been destiny.

I later went to Yale when Barbara Bush was there
Wasn't that the coincidence?
Grampa and I both mingled with royalty
We crossed a mighty fence.

Years later, they cornered me in the hospital
And told me it was because of Grampa
Right there I knew the Navy
Had gotten itself an imposter.

I won't say it was a former President
With revenge for the resurrected Geronimo
I'll say it was just a dream
And watch you lose the show.

Pantomime

The air was thinning out
And he saw his reflection
A bitter man with bitter ways
Far from the resurrection.

He kept his identity secret
For decades at a time
The only ones who saw him
Ended up dead like a piece of slime.

Except this one little trooper
She clamored on for years
Sometimes writing poetry
Other times swallowing tears.

But he became obsessed with the mother
In part because of looks
Another part was her heavy mouth
She would rock him with her "shooks."

He felt insecure around her
But vowed to fight for her honor
What entity did this to her?
A beauty but now a goner!

She told him it was her father
Signed the papers for electric shock
That's all he needed to hear
Someone to hate, someone to clock.

Never did he consider
It wasn't her father's fault
The Psychiatrist convinced him
It had to do with salt.

So, one day when he was older
He vowed to get him back
The man who could do no wrong
Was now down for the attack.

He let him fall down the stairs
And it caused a heart commotion
That's for shocking my wife
He said with a daring potion.

Miraculously, the man recovered
With a special cheerleader at his side
Getting him to breathe through the plastic
By reciting the Yankee players, one at a time.

Breathe this breath for Jeter
Next one for Matsui
She yelled like a coach
At homecoming with Uncle Louie.

He was safe for a while
But it became his time
Had enough of your smells and sounds
I could see his pantomime.

Then one day when the coast was clear
He allowed the man in to finish the job
It was one way he got back at him
For making his daughter look like a slob.

Bullying

She sets her clothes out neatly
And always combs her hair
Anything to minimize insult
From 4th graders who don't care.

She changed schools to give it a try
And at first things were going well
She made a few close friends
And thought things were really swell.

But little by little it began to change
The bullying set right in
You're not one of our kind
And your skin is way too thin.

We will call you names
Like "white girl," "fat," and "skunk"
We will pull your hair out
And treat you like a punk.

You thought you'd be part of us?
Because your blood is mixed?
We will stick with each other
And fight you with our bricks.

If you tell the teacher
We'll call you a real bad snitch
If you get me suspended
I'll throw you in a ditch!

Back in the day we might have
Told her to straight up fight
She's six inches taller than them
And packs a punch with very good might.

But we must raise our girls to be "civil"
And take in all these words
Suck it up cause we're privileged?
No matter how much we hurt?

This was one such school
And I have just about had it
Going back to where my girl was supported
To stop her tears so tragic.

But a lesson to all the parents
Your children may seem fine
But the day you get that lump in your throat
Your heart will be breaking just like mine.

Who's Man

Mommy, do you have some time?
I have a question to ask
Someone said my skin makes me bad
And I'd better wear a mask.

They said my skin is evil
From things done years ago
They told me I'm an oppressor
And that I really should just go.

The land belongs to Natives
And whites were not here first
So, anyone wishing to stay
Will end up in a hearse.

But where can we go, Mama?
Will It'ly take us back?
What about our Italian side?
Weren't we once considered Black?

Yes, we were, sweet darling
And that's an important lesson to learn
Skin color is a social construction
You can glorify it or let it burn.

But what's inside is priceless
And as long as you don't judge
I dare any hard nose in this world
To try to make you budge.

For at that time and mark my words
If this is the ultimate plan
You will see this world in a different light
Our true friends will stand up and show who's man.

Ridiculous

Columbus was an original colonizer
Even though he worked for Spain
You all still blame Italians
Want to guilt us for this stain.

Once again, your points are classless
For Italian peasants took no part
All we did was get kicked out of Italy
Only to find your careless cold heart.

And like the poor white English
Who were thrown in abandoned hulks[99]
Some would like us Italians all in prison
So, they could judge with disdain and sulk.

Do you know how many poor Italian men?
End up in jails and prisons?
No, they don't report on ethnicity
Or class with any kind of precision.

Over half of the prison population
Happens to be white[100]
Although racism is fierce
That number isn't slight.

You'd think by now we'd have the key
To escape the cruel cold bars
But we still get chased around
No matter our internal scars.

---

[99] Duckworth, J. (2002). *Fagin's Children: Criminal Children in Victorian England.* Bloomsbury Publishing. See also Slack, P. (1995). *The English Poor Law, 1531-1782* (No. 9). Cambridge University Press.

[100] Federal Bureau of Prisons. (2023). *BOP Statistics: Inmate Race.* Retrieved from https://www.bop.gov/about/statistics/statistics_inmate_race.jsp

If you'd like to know what to do now
I'd say to read an old paper[101]
In it I suggest a model that I believe in
Perhaps it can be picked up by the Lakers.

The government may not fund a program
If it can't show results through statistics
I don't know about you all
But I find this all rather ridiculous.

---

[101] Bryan, J. L., Haldipur, J., Martin, M., & Ullrich, S. (2015). Envisioning a broader role for philanthropy in prison reform. *Society, 52*(6), 572-579.

Comply

I remember in "Dear Mama"[102]
When Tupac's mom spoke
She was so happy to have a boy
And all that it would invoke.

For me, I felt the opposite
Jumped up six-feet off the table spur
When they said my first was a girl
I thought maybe now they'd let me keep her.

Then at the age of 41
In came the most astonishing news
God blessed us with another miracle
She was a gift, no way we could lose.

We went to the hospital for a scan
And they looked up my old record
Saw a history of bipolar in the computer
Said "you shouldn't have a second."

The hospital staff ordered every test
Tried to talk me out of having Gianna
Do you want to chance mental illness?
Why not abort the "cells" and take a sauna?

My husband and I formed an alliance
We would not listen to their threats
We put our faith in the Lord and prayed
Gianna came through with some heavy sweat.

Then when it came time for my release
They handed me a white envelope
Said give this to the pediatrician
They tried to play me out as dope.

In the letter was a special note
In all caps and red underlining
This patient has a bipolar history

---

[102] Shakur, T. (1995) Dear Mama. On *Me Against the World* [Album]. Interscope, Jive

Make sure you start your spying.

Though I was hurt beyond repair
I lowered my humiliated face
Handed the letter to the doctor
Prepared to be disgraced.

They didn't say anything
But every time I go there
I must have my kids looking tip-top in shape
Heaven forbid they pull them from my care.

Funny how I thought HIPAA
Protected me from airing out laundry
Guess that rule doesn't apply to me
They love to call me "sick" and taunt me.

I went home and listened all night
To songs by the Lost Boyz and Lil' Wayne
Cried my heart out to "Renee"[103] and "How to Love"[104]
Tried to ease my deep gut-wrenching pain.

Even though I was wrongly labeled
I cannot fight that scar
I must take the medicine and gain tons of weight
So, I'm not such a threat to the star.

Then maybe they'll let me raise
My children with some pride
Hoping they can't be removed
As long as I dutifully comply.

---

[103] Kelly, T & Archer, D. (1996). Renee. [Recorded by Lost Boyz]. On *Legal Drug Money* [Album]. Uptown.

[104] Carter Jr., D., Boyd. M., Seymour, L., Seymour, L., Preyan, J., & Fisher, N. (2011). How to Love [Recorded by Lil' Wayne]. On *Tha Carter IV* [Album]. Young Money, Cash Money, Universal Republic

My Song

The saddest day of my life
Was when I visited my first-born daughter
At a child welfare agency
Because of the damn distorter.

They tried to school my husband
On their evil plan
"If ever Jenn acts out of step
Just throw her in the can."

You just need one phone call
And she'll shudder at the thought
She'll remember all that happened
The day her life was bought.

Well, in the hospital I landed
And in walks "Lottie Dottie"[105]
Looks at me with disdain
Asks me to go "pee pee on the potty."

Another lovely nurse comes in
Are you feeling "mad, glad, or sad?"
Like I'm a two-year-old
They listened to my stepdad.

I usually say very little
Because I find it all rather futile
Sometimes I argue back
And it becomes even more brutal.

But this one day my heart was broken
My husband and I were fighting
I had to visit my daughter
As child welfare workers kept me in their sighting.

---

[105] Smith, J.T. (1987). Get Down [Recorded by LL Cool J]. On *Bigger and Deffer* [Album].L.A. Posse.

I brought in a Minnie Mouse ball
And intended on us both playing
But when my little one saw me
She ran to me without delaying.

I started singing a song I made for her
When she was growing in my womb
We stayed "heart-to-heart" for ten straight minutes
And the worker felt my doom.

"Angeliiiiiia, your mama loves you"
I sang it over and over again
I tried to fight back the tears
I wanted her to see me on the mend.

The worker saw something wasn't quite right
How could I be crazy and work these good jobs?
How could I be a danger?
She couldn't take my dolphin-like sobs.

Well, my boss took up for me
Wrote me a real nice letter
Said this is all a big mistake
Suggested they make it better.

And the worker began to see
It was not I who was a danger
Though they couldn't prove it
They saw through my family's anger.

Still, it taught me a lesson
Never accuse my family of anything wrong
If I do, they'll come after me
They don't want me to sing my song.

Guaranteed

There are books about being Black
In what is called "white space"[106]
Well, I've always been the white
Working hard for the Black race.

From the very beginning
I've worked hard for the cause
But now some whites said I'm not needed no more
Got kicked out by a powerful white woman with applause.

Consistently asked to tell my trauma
But still judged for resembling bleach
They give me a whole two minutes
I audition in an elevator speech.

They make me degrade myself
So, they can feel they are above
It's a common micro-aggression
That hides right under the cuff.

Twenty-five years in social justice
I always have to start from jump
Never can I get a nod of credence
Always have to work from a slump.

I don't know where some get off
The people prefer to tell me their story
They don't trust half of you snot rags
You're the ones who made them sorry.

---

[106] Anderson, E. (2022). *Black in White Space: The Enduring Impact of Color in Everyday Life*. University of Chicago Press. See also Pinkett, R. D., Robinson, J. A., & Patterson, P. (2010). *Black Faces in White Places: 10 Game-Changing Strategies to Achieve Success and Find Greatness*. Amacom. See also Fanon, F. (2008). *Black Skin, White Masks*. Grove Press.

But like Venkatesh in *Gang Leader*[107]
True street people take me under their wing
It's only the stuffy Black and white folks
Who don't want me to be the one to sing.

They want to be the ones
The ones to save the hood
Even though their messages are harmful
They smile wide as they're up to no good.

You can't correct the harms of racism
By only looking at statistical variables
You need people with "lived experience"
To help resolve what's wrong with parables.

"Credible messengers" are indeed important
To that I certainly agree
But let an old Mafia boss talk to them
They would all listen, guaranteed.

---

[107] Venkatesh, S. A. (2008). *Gang Leader for a Day: A Rogue Sociologist Takes to the Streets.* Penguin.

Race

I worked on a prisoner reentry evaluation
I was the one to do interviews
But the leader didn't like my skin color
She was supposed to be the only white in the room.

So, she asked me to tell my story
And then fed it to the crowd
She wanted them to challenge my experience
She wanted them to throw me out.

I kept my composure
For clearly, I needed the job
This white woman was powerful
But I still stepped to that snob.

She told me she protested the Vietnam war
And I disclosed that my uncle served
She didn't like my counterpoint
Made sure to get me unnerved.

This woman talked to my boss and she
Started treating me differently
Said I talked too "colloquially"
Very unlike my professional degree.

I said that country part of me comes from my grampa
And she didn't seem to understand the point
She said I needed to "up" my "public-facing-speak"
Never realizing my family's been in the joint.

You can't win if you talk regular
You can't win if you talk white
But the next thing that happened there
Was really, really not right.

They asked me to join a mystery mug exchange
And I picked a woman who didn't like me
Still, I tried to do everything
To purchase a mug that she'd find striking.

She gave some hints on what she wanted
She said she liked "nature and art"
I purchased a mug with an African American woman
Artistically dancing in a nature-like park.

The next day I got called into the office
My boss and my co-worker were there
Both women were clearly unhappy
They gave me the keen old stare.

My coworker picked up the mug
And turned it upside down
Said "This says African American expressions"
That's not your part of town.

She told me there was a "white section" of Hallmark
And that I crossed into the Black
She told me she identified as Afro-Latina
I was down for the white-collar attack.

I asked her if she liked the mug
She said she did indeed
I asked her what the problem was
She said she didn't want anything from me.

My boss asked me to apologize
But my coworker refused my hand
She got up and walked right out
She wanted to make *me* her stand.

I started crying instantly
And then went to HR
To be accused of a micro-aggression?
After all I've been through in this spar?

Suffice is to say it's not always easy
It's not always easy to be white in Black space
But some would never consider that
Cause they're just focused on their own race.

Pick up the pace.

People and Places

She met him many years ago
And might was what she saw
Never before in her life
Had she met someone so like paw.

She wondered if he caught a glimpse
Or if it was out of pity
That he accepted a young ghetto girl into Yale
You know her from Jersey City.

People are places and places become people
Is what she'd like to say
Just give them a passage from Doreen Massey[108]
And let them have it their way.

It is a shame that people do not realize
They should reach out to someone unlike themselves
To see what they have in common
To help heal their fragmented selves.

I'm sure an African American man
Could listen to my family's story
Tell us not to be so petty
And live together in glory.

And then one day after
Italians can do the same
We can meet with African Americans
And share who we have to blame.

Figure out what we have in common
And forge a brand-new order
Stay divided as we are
And end up out of use like an old video recorder.

---

[108] Massey, D. (2008). A global sense of place. In *The Cultural Geography Reader* (pp. 269-275). Routledge.

Ukraine

I thought of you today
As I made your favorite breakfast
Farina with some milk
Is enough to leave one breathless.

I wish that I could reach out
Host you in my home
We haven't much to offer
But we can build us a modest dome.

I've seen you had to pack up
And leave your treasures behind
I imagine that made you very sad
Like the splinter bleeding my mind.

I wish you strength and kindness
I wish you Solomon's prayer
Get those stinking invaders
And kick them out of there.[109]

---

[109] As is suggested throughout this book, the conflict between Russia and Ukraine, like many conflicts, is fueled by propaganda about what each side has done, or plans to do, to their brother. With such images and rhetoric neatly outlined, some cannot seem to help taking on such beliefs. For a discussion of the current Russian war on Ukraine, please see Etkind, A. (2022). Ukraine, Russia, and genocide of minor differences. *Journal of Genocide Research*, 1-19. See also Fortuin, E. (2022). Ukraine commits genocide on Russians: The term "genocide" in Russian propaganda. *Russian Linguistics*, 46(3), 313-347.

Rumblings of Genocide

Rumblings of genocide
In my ear
Rumblings of genocide
Hold me dear.

Rumblings of genocide
You have nothing to fear
Rumblings of genocide
You're in the clear.

Rumblings of genocide
They've changed the look
Rumblings of genocide
Leo Kuper's book.[110]

Rumblings of genocide
Now it's our turn
Rumblings of genocide
Will we burn?

Rumblings of genocide
Did you stick up for others?
Rumblings of genocide
Did you treat people as brothers?

Rumblings of genocide
We are too fair
Rumblings of genocide
Doesn't anyone care?

Rumblings of genocide
See you there
Rumblings of genocide
Only if you dare.

---

[110] Kuper, L. (1981). *Genocide: Its Political Use in the Twentieth Century.* Yale University Press.

Memories to Save

Memories long forsaken
Is what I strive to reveal
Hoping that you'll tap in
Perhaps I can remind you how to feel.

I wish I could just be myself
And reach out to all mankind
But they will not accept me now
My skin is too thin to find.

I will still write my poems
And hope your exterior begins to cave
For sturdy arms can hold the farms
But I am the one to save.

The Marching Crowd

Your infinite is now finite
The day is coming near
Your book lay on the shelf
Contemplating fear.

The man of whom you spoke
Was closer than you thought
Your loved one married him
That's how your life was bought.

I warned you about Sabrina
I warned you about the waters
You took some heat for following
But your heart had other orders.

And now you're in the corner
Like a college kid playing quarters
Working like a trucker
To raise two beautiful daughters.

I won't say I'm sorry
I know you don't need that
I'll mend what I have broken
The kid will get the cat.

But in my lonely travels
May I say that I am proud?
You had the courage to stand up
And reverse the marching crowd.

My Pup

I'm conflicted as I write this
Unsure if anyone cares
My days of cheerful dancing
Have slowed like a crawl up the stairs.

I have two children and a family
And need to remain close-lipped
Still the energy I'm feeling
Is like the wings of a bird unclipped.

I cannot write as freely
I only hope I've reached a few
The years are violet-silver skies
With messages sent on cue.

I wish you all good fortune
And luck from the good Lord's cup
I'm bowing out of the contest
And passing to my pup.

Favoritism

Dear Professor, I have a question to ask
Do I say that I'm straight and bring in a flask?
Do I bow on all fours to just let them know?
I'm not a racist or anti-gay, but here is your show?

My dear sweet students
You know who you are
Don't let anyone judge you
Or put you in a car.

I know your hearts
You're very good people
It's just academics
Trying to deceive you.

But what about work?
Will there be any for us?
That I can't promise
Been like this for months.

There is favoritism
I'm sorry, it's true
And if you watch very closely
You'll see it too.

Voluntary Immigration

We walked at night and cried
We wandered through the dark
We were not afraid of it
We just needed a landmark.

Brother, can you spare some change?
That was our most desperate
The rest huddled like soldiers
And pieced together rent checks.

Aunt Lena signed hers right over
When mom needed a docta
What's a paycheck between gumas?
When you're workin' for the pasta?!

You can take my olives
Maybe let me hold your onions
See if Anna has some cheese
And we can meet Paul Bunyan.[111]

Meet Paul Bunyan? That's in books
You really believe that's true
We're Paesanas ol' gumadas
They won't see us through.

Why they won't see you
You don't have a voice?
Yes, but we've been told
We did have us a choice.

Academics like Mary Waters[112]
Said ethnicity for whites is an option
She made fun of our ethnic dishes
And traipsed on us like a python.

---

[111] Dorson, R. M. (1977). *American Folklore: With Revised Bibliographical Notes, 1977* (Vol. 4). University of Chicago Press.

[112] Waters, M. C. (1990). *Ethnic Options: Choosing Identities in America*. University of California Press. See also Steinberg, S. (2001). *The Ethnic Myth: Race, Ethnicity, and Class in America*. Beacon Press.

But her variables were atrocious
Never once did she fully account for
All the Italians who changed their names
Or got nose jobs to escape the scorn.

She didn't travel to Marion
Or better yet to Staten Island
For that would make her claim erroneous
She never understood the life of a paisan!

Furthermore, there is the immigrant trauma
Branded within our DNA
We can feel what our ancestors went through
And it messes up our day.

Still, academia spread the word
That ethnicity or culture is not important for us
We got whittled down to just "white status" [113]
Along with the "Medigans" who hurt us.

And through it we had no choice
We thought we were Italian
But they want to diminish our story
And take off with our medallion.

---

[113] For an explanation of Italians and "whiteness," please see Guglielmo, J., & Salerno, S. (Eds.). (2012). *Are Italians White?: How Race is Made in America*. Routledge.

Mezzogiorno

I took a class at NYU
Because Yale didn't focus on urban
Harvey was the professor
And he rarely kept us hurtin.'

I learned about use value
And exchange is how they work
He and Logan wrote a good book[114]
But did they know about the jerk?

Making Democracy Work[115]
Robert Putnam wrote that book
In it he painted Southern Italians as low lives
And within me was I shook.

I felt a certain kind of angry-blood flow
And the professor surely felt it
Did you feel rage, dear student?
Yes, I wanted to tear off his head and welt it.

For in this book is no mention
Of how the Northern Italians controlled class
Southern Italians were the scapegoats
Just look at Cesare Lombroso and his sorry ass.[116]

The father of Eugenics was really
A wealthy Jewish-Italian man who hated below the Mezzogiorno
His message spread about Southern Italy
Was used against the American "Negro."[117]

---

[114] Logan, J. R., Molotch, H. L., & Molotch, H. (2007). *Urban fortunes: The political economy of place*. Univ of California Press.

[115] Putnam, R. D., Leonardi, R., & Nanetti, R. Y. (1992). *Making democracy work: Civic traditions in modern Italy*. Princeton university press.

[116] Pick, D. (2017). The faces of anarchy: Lombroso and the politics of criminal science in post-unification Italy. In *European Political History 1870–1913* (pp. 351-377). Routledge. See also Caglioti, A. M. (2017). Race, statistics and Italian eugenics: Alfredo Niceforo's trajectory from Lombroso to fascism (1876–1960). *European History Quarterly*, *47*(3), 461-489.

[117] Lombroso, C. (2006). Criminal man. In *Criminal Man*. Duke University Press.

And that is what we share in common
The process of being blood-labeled[118]
But some would never know this history
Cause they only care about their own being disabled.

---

[118] Mezzano, M. J. (2009). *"Not The Race of Dante": Southern Italians as undesirable Americans* (dissertation). Boston College, Boston, MA.

Fragility

Let me ask you a question
If a woman has been raped?
Does her tragic story not matter?
If another was raped and maimed?

If one woman was raped and killed?
But another was "only" tortured and raped?
Does that make her trauma less than?
Can you not absorb the charade?

Apply this lesson to race
And this is what I'm saying
Italians had it pretty bad
But we have no way of complaining.

We were told we had Black blood
And our inner hearts were violent
We are shown as psychotic mobsters[119]
Never once do you hear our silence!

Before you go and twist my words
Let me make it clear
Slavery against African Americans
Was certainly worse than any here.

But does that mean Italians have no story?
About what happened to our people?
Does that mean we get cast out?
Is your mind really just that feeble?

You sit in your academic classroom
And scream out "you can't compare!"
You read about white fragility[120]
And think you know the scare.

---

[119] Coppola, F. F. (1972). *The Godfather, The Godfather II, The Godfather III,* Paramount Pictures; Scorsese, M. (1990). Goodfellas. Warner Bros.; De Niro, R. (1993). A Bronx Tale. Savoy Pictures; Brad Grey Television production in association with HBO original programming. *(1999). The Sopranos. [New York, N.Y.] :HBO*

[120] DiAngelo, R. (2018). *White fragility: Why it's so hard for white people to talk about racism.* Beacon Press.

But let me give you a dare
Step one day in my shoes with their snare
And you'll find you cannot bear
The harsh reality of my chair.

Oh where.

String and Ball

Pop, I was thinking
What do they think?
We came over here
To make a big stink?

No, we come over heah
To make uh dee money
Causa in Italia
Dey stop uh de honey.

But what do they do?
When they want us out?
How do they do it?
With a fist or a pout?

No, dey stot it wit uh
"A u no wothy
All you do is eat and a u
Kids is always dirty."

Well, how can they blame you?
If the country doesn't provide?
I mean isn't it a crime?
Like slow-death homicide?

No, de no see likea data
I wish dey would
Den we no have it so many
Problems in uh de hood.

Yeah, but Pop they come back
Now they're over here
What do we do?
Pull them by the ear?

No, you justa pray
Nicea Nicea and all
And a u watchit go away
Wid uh string and uh ball.

Waiting for Recognition

I waited many years
For a sign of recognition
Not something politically sound
But about the resurrection.

I didn't know if you saw me
And pretended to turn away
Out of twisted protection
To make it through another day.

I didn't know if you missed me
When traveling toward greener grass
I didn't know if you'd approve
Of my work with the working class.

I just wanted some inkling of closure
Something to say "well done"
Not the fake and phony brand
But from someone who's taken a gun.

Bad Boy

I met him many years ago
He was a professor at Yale
I practically worshiped his every word
But he still left me alone, stale.

He told his friends he found someone
Who could reach beyond their looks
Someone whose writing could shake loose
The crookedest of all crooks.

His friends were from the land of rye
And asked how much does she cost?
She writes for free is what he said
And her family is rather lost.

They don't know who she really is
In fact, they think she's crazy
That will work in our favor
Plus, her husband's lazy.

What do you want from her?
Is all the people asked
I want her to suffer insanity
For all my people she tasked.

She could have stopped WWII
And the entire baseless cost
But she decided to fly away
And leave us tempest-tossed.

What makes you think she flew away?
And didn't suffer in that awful camp?
What makes you think she left you alone?
Without a candle or a lamp?

She tried to explain the problem to you
So, you could lead your people
But you chose to step on her some more
Take it out on the steeple.

Now that your days are slowing down
Tell me how does it feel?
To know how much damage you caused?
Because you refuse to heal?

Well, I won't fault you at all
You played the game real well
Even invented yourself as Q
Put a list together to sell.

You got the people to trust in you
Because you know what they fear
And then you did as you always do
Found a way to disappear.

And now we're in a boat again
While you're playing coy
If I didn't know any better
I'd say you're a real bad boy.

Avenging World War II

I have my confirmation
I know just what you've done
I can't say I'm surprised
You gave it away with your cowboy son.

From the moment the officer told me:
"It was someone close who got you on that list"
Your face flashed before my eyes
And the visions would only persist.

I understand you saw me as a threat
In that I can sway a group
But why tell me to focus on Muslims?
And then set me up for a coup?

Why call the FBI?
Why send my confidential field notes?
Why tell Skull and Bones?
She's the one now slit her throat?

It is because you are a bad man
And bad men will never be
They will never cross the Jericho
They will never erase Crocodile Dundee.[121]

But my goodness how you've tried
To test the law of Job
You underestimated the ghetto
Like the Emperor and his robe.[122]

Tell me, just what did you get?
By trying to silence me?
You're now dealing with an army
That bows down to eternity.

---

[121] Crofts, S. (1989). Re-imaging Australia: Crocodile Dundee overseas. *Continuum: Journal of Media & Cultural Studies, 2*(2), 129-142.

[122] Bash, A. (2004). Spirituality: the emperor's new clothes?. *Journal of Clinical Nursing, 13*(1), 11-16.

I was much more middle-grounded
Reaching out to far extremes
But you preferred to knock me
Leave me reeling from the seams.

Now your days are ending
And you're finding more to do
Leaving without a trace
Will never happen to you.

Curiosity might need to kill the cat
And satisfaction will likely bring him back
But you brought drugs to the ghetto
To try to thwart off an attack.

You praised HIV
You minimized 911
And you think your pristine reputation?
Will get you into Heaven?

Once again, you thought real wrong
Lombroso can't lay off the Italian boat
That's why one day soon
He'll meet up with a Croat.

And when that Croat asks him
Just what has he done?
He'll quickly recall the conversation
And think about the one.

The war in Yugoslavia[123]
Will be seen as crystal clear
They went there because of Medjugorje[124]
And whispered in their ear.

---

[123] Oberschall, A. (2000). The manipulation of ethnicity: from ethnic cooperation to violence and war in Yugoslavia. *Ethnic and racial studies, 23*(6), 982-1001. See also MacDonald, D. B. (2003). *Balkan Holocausts?: Serbian and Croatian victim centred propaganda and the war in Yugoslavia.* Manchester University Press.

[124] Pandarakalam, J. P. (2001). Are the apparitions of Medjugorje real. *Journal of Scientific Exploration, 15*(2), 229-239.

They showed pictures of Serbs
Being killed by Muslim hands
They showed the Croats similar ones
Knowing they doctored up all the strands.

And then there is old Putin
He's in with him too
Avenging World War II
Is all they seek to do.

911

On the morning of 911
I got this feeling in my gut
It said "get out now"
And I ran out with a strut.

I was waiting for Grampa
To drive me to the PATH
I'd take the World Trade Center train
And then ride the subway math.

But this feeling in my gut
Was more than I could bear
I couldn't wait for Grampa
I had to get the hell out of there.

So, I jumped in my mom's green dodge
I borrowed it the night before
My car overheated
Had it towed to a mechanic's door.

My mom made me swear
I would not take her car to New York
Right there I should have known
She was warning me about the dork.

She had a secret way
Of sensing things going wrong
Like the summer before 911
She called 411 300 times to sing her song.

Meanwhile that summer at Columbia University
My boss met with top leaders
Michael Bloomberg was campaigning[125]
And she became one of his cheerleaders.

---

[125] For an ethnography of the effects of Stop and Frisk, please see Haldipur, J. (2018). *No place on the corner: The costs of aggressive policing*. NYU Press. For an analysis of how Michael Bloomberg changed positions by donating to Black Lives Matter, please see Welch, M. (2015). Black Lives Matter and Michael Bloomberg: the oddest couple? *Los Angeles Times*. For a note on the 9/11 Michael Bloomberg/Mark Green Mayoral

She was an expert on mayoral politics[126]
And Bloomberg was her man
Though she couldn't consult from the center
She still found a way to help the plan.

But on that day of 911
I felt a heavy weight
I drove down Observer Highway
Right through the red light and tunnel gate.

I saw the man in the glass box
He was nervously waving his hand
I felt proud that I went through the light
Against his grave command.

Then inside the Holland Tunnel
I got another really strange sense
I peeked in the rear-view mirror
Only five cars were behind me, tense.

Then as soon as I neared the New York opening
I felt the whole world tilted to the left
I saw the first ball of orange flames
The tower was a mess.

I pulled over on the West Side Highway
And the car behind me stopped
On the other side of the highway
Was a sea of fire engines, ambulances, and cops.

I knew this was something big
So, I tried to call home
But my cell battery died
I couldn't call my clone.

I turned on 1010 wins
And the man said he saw the first plane hit
He was at the Empire State building

---

race, please see Kraus, J. (2004). Mark Green and the collapse of the urban democratic coalition. *Politics & Policy, 32*(2), 201-221.

[126] Fuchs, E. R., & Fuchs, F. (1992). *Mayors and money: Fiscal policy in New York and Chicago.* University of Chicago Press.

And I wondered how he saw it.

When I arrived at work at Columbia
I was like Chicken Little[127] in a fit
I told what I had seen
But also, how my insides twitched.

One professor looked at me sympathetically
As though he knew a secret I didn't know
He told me "I can't put you up"
And I thought that was really strange ego.

Why would I need to be put up?
I guess he knew the story
I almost couldn't get home that day
But then crossed the GW bridge with glory.

My sister met me up at work
And the whole work crew got some pizza
I could not eat a single thing
I pulled dusty blue binders down from the bleachers.

On the Jersey side of the Hudson
All you could see
Was a cloud-like wave of smoke
From the towers to Columbia University.

Immediately that day
I went to visit my grandparents
Made sure they were ok
Everyone was frantic.

Later on, that night
I went to downtown Jersey City to visit the scene
I could not believe the towers
Disappeared so clean.

The towers were like friends to Jersey City
Locals felt honored to have the best view
With a crystal-clear view of the damage
It felt like they were taken from us, true.

---

[127] Emberley, R., & Emberley, E. (2009). *Chicken little*. Macmillan.

All that was left was smoke and flames
And a very odd scent of curry
I gathered the oil from the planes
Was burned off in a hurry.

I was glued to the news
Watching people looking for loved ones
I hoped the people would find
More of their missing sons.

Then on October 7, 2001
I went to visit Grampa at Wallis
Gave him my hat from ground zero
And asked him to help me resolve this.

Grampa, I want to write my dissertation
On what happens after 911
Will the community become divided?
Or look to make this Heaven?

Grampa gave me a compassionate squeeze
If you want to know about 911
Go to the Mosque on West side
Find out about the Leven.

And so, to the Mosque I went
My professors at Yale all approved it
Later on, it would come back to bite me
When I became unsuited.

Although I told my Muslim participants
I was writing about "the true"
They laughed with a knowing smile
"We know it was Allah who sent you."

Too Illicit

After 911, working at Columbia
Wasn't the same
By chance, I wore a scapula on that day
And they all took note of my name.

They offered me a grant to go home
And work on my dissertation
For some reason they didn't want me there
I guess it had to do with my station.

Columbia had a "Muslims in New York City" project
And I organized a nice pre-911 conference
Brought in leaders from all over
Worked to build trust in grave confidence.

But some didn't want Muslims
To start taking over
Needed to develop a plan
To "pop one in the shoulder."[128]

My boss sent me to Brooklyn
And they asked if I was a Jew
At the time I didn't know my DNA
So, I said "no" really cool.

The group was deciding on what to rebuild
And one man suggested an underwater bridge
From New York City to Jersey City
People could walk through with their kids.

I thought that was a cool idea
But said the towers should be rebuilt the same
For some reason they didn't want them up there
They wanted elongated triangles to mark their claim.

---

[128] Myrick, N., Tyson, R., Sigler, W., Carter, S. (1997) You Must Love Me. [Recorded by Jay-Z] On *In My Lifetime, VOL. 1.* Def Jam, Roc-A-Fella

They came up with the "Freedom Tower"
And I still cannot get myself to visit
Knowing something's not quite right
Makes the trip too illicit.

Still, I miss it.

Icebox

What holds me together
Is that I'm Neapolitan
Predicting the future
Like Nos Tra Dam.

The man wanted his father
To outlive the best man
That's why he shot in
With his sick plan.

His father died at 94
And that was his pride
Didn't want to see Grampa
Make the year 95.

So, he preached and he preached
To his bee hive
Told them Grampa's ancestors
Once strapped his behind.

He even paid dude
To pull a gun on my stepfather
While working at CVS
Made it look like a squatter.

But I know the deal
His brain's in a fog
Take him to London
Let him leap like a frog.

Take him on tour
As though he were a performer
Like the Sorrento dancers
Make him work for a quarter.

Do it swiftly
Or slow it down
Take him around the world
Show him off like a clown.

Then frown
With a side-eye shot at his lapel
Ask him if it was all worth
The beat of the missile.

And if he says swell
Just hold onto your gel
You can't shake that evil man
He was born in a cell.

If you try to get him to yell
He'll make a face as you swell
Your plan will go no further
Than an icebox in hell.

Feather

I know what went down in Georgia
In case it is not clear
I know you saw me as an enemy
And favored my husband, so dear.

I will not go after you
I will let you fall
You listened to the devil's sermon
You ought to have known the brawl.

You claim to be about "the people"
When I heard you lecture on anti-gay
Now that politically it's in favor
Why, you'll support them on this day!

You can sit around and play Priestess
But you'll never be canonized
For you only care about avenging your own
We can see right through your lies.

Now read a book by Ulf Hannerz[129]
And piece his critics together
What you long for in this world
Is right here in my ink-filled feather.

---

[129] Hannerz, U. (1968). The rhetoric of soul: Identification in Negro society. *Race*, 9(4), 453-465. See also Hannerz, U. (1974). Ethnicity and opportunity. *Urban Ethnicity.* London: Tavistock, 37-76.

Shame

You think today's videos are sexy?
Half-dressed girls and fancy cars?
Just look to *Very Young Girls*[130]
See how the pimp life has them scarred.

This is supposed to be our children
But we leave them all alone
Put on a robe for Ruth Bader Ginsberg?
While very young girls have no home?

You think Malcom X would go for it?
What about Martin Luther King?
I may be stepping on some toes
But for young girls I'll meet you in the ring.

You want to make a difference?
Reach out to Rachel Lloyd
Give her some money for housing
Help get those girls employed.

I'm asking you to stop the hurt feelings
I'm asking you to catch up to the game
The free love movement we are into
Is what puts many young girls to shame.

Look at what you're falling for
Do you really want kids to see such images?
What the hell happened to your chastity?
Don't let them blow away your faithful lineage!

---

[130] Schisgall, D., & Alvarez, N. (Directors). (2007). *Very Young Girls* [Film]. Showtime.

Darryl

Scheming like an Accountant
On April 14th
How many more suckers
Can I beat off the streets?

Well, you can read 'em and weep
My soul's on fire, that deep
You can't shame my family
We fight to prepare for the steep.

But you call
The police
I sit with all this knowledge
Never once do I squeak.

You wait on my turn
Like a fatal gas leak
Still, you're weak
And a sneak.

I raise your soul, bleak
Maybe you can call your mother
And stop the cold speak
But we know you want just to wreak
Havoc on my invisible widow's peak.

Well, I don't know what to tell ya
I'm fresh out of guesses
Maybe try your brother
He's into head dresses.

As for me I'll be looking out
For who I can hold
With my other brother Darryl[131]
I'll make the demon fold.

---

[131] Kemp, B., Egan, M., Solomon, M., Wilcox, D., Wyman, D., & Mirkin, D. (Executive Producers). (1982-1990). *Newhart* [TV series]. CBS.

Missalettes

I searched for the one person
Responsible for so much pain
While you all aim at low hanging fruit
Drink some liquor and complain.

The one crowned took a trip
To confirm his own birth right
While you all sit and wait
He takes what's in his sight.

Physically, he's an Adonis
They selected the best looking one
Sat left of me in a restorative justice circle
So, I could pass him my baton.

My friends, it does not work like that
You cannot trick me out of my pass
You can only meet me at Church
Take out your missalettes – it's time for mass.

That Dance

My friend, how the hell are ya?
My, it's been some time
Since someone whispered in your ear
"I found the one, now make her mine."

It was at a Conference at Columbia
A month before 911
She reached out to the Director
"That program coordinator, is she from Heaven?"

I was just a young girl
Innocent as could be
I walked around the University
Trying to fix poverty.

But you, you couldn't have it
A poor girl who went to Yale
Why, she'd fit our secret vision!
Lock her up and leave no bail!

Wait, now just a minute
Why should we lock her up?
What about psychological torture?
Would that fill your cup?

No, I want her to bleed
For permitting a hollow cause
I want her only to suffer
And do not give her a pause.

Years went by and what happened?
Did you ever successfully plan my death?
Each time you attempted
Had me looking like I was on meth.

Crazy and wide-eyed
Because I could sense the hit
Meanwhile you sit pretty
Cow down and swallow your spit.

But tell me, my friend
Just how does it feel?
To know that it was one of your own?
Who tipped me off to your appeal?

He was magical in his delivery
Just like the man from above
He showed up in my office
And presented as a white dove.

He told me about the vision
He told me about the curse
He told me someone would be after me
He warned me about the purse.

He told me some Jewish folks believe
That the returned-Jesus would go to Yale
It was a legend they hold onto closely
And hoped it wouldn't fail.

He was one of the finest Jewish people
And man, did he take a chance!
I wonder why I haven't seen him
Did you kill him for that dance?

Te Brute

I understand you feel unready
And not sure of your path
I see that you are weary
From eons full of wrath.

But if you could just trust in me
I will not steer you wrong
You are the one we waited for
And now I'll sing your song.

Once upon a child
Once upon a day
You walked with wondrous spirit
And meaning led your way.

But then you saw a bitter world
One you'd hardly recognize
How could you make a dent in this?
And still manage to survive?

How could you both make your mark?
And give back to the Lord?
For saving you from that awful place
You still cannot bear to hear its chord.

Maybe you'll just walk on by
And they won't see you, Skip
They'll just think of you as a grandpa
And you'll get by without a drip.

But nosy academics
Wouldn't let you have your peace
Following you around the world
Like Mary and her fleece.[132]

---

[132] Trapani, I. (2013). *Mary Had a Little Lamb*. Charlesbridge.

Well, you can keep your privacy
I do not fault you for that
But when you sold me out to them
That's where I fell oh so flat.

You're a lofty man with lofty goals
And international zeal galore
But you left your young ethnographer
To die before the age of 34.

For as the legend had it
Kill at 33
Then you won't transition
From Jesus of Galilee.

Some academics were onto you
They saw your work as pure
Could he be the "risen son?"
Hiding behind the door?

But you were not quite comfortable
With the attention you received
For the legend of Jesus going to Yale
Was one you too believed.

But you didn't want to take on that clout
For you knew how it would end
With your family chased and followed
As crosses burn, my friend.

So, what did you decide, old mentor?
Tell me, just what did you do?
You passed my name along to your team
And watched it all come true.

But now that I hath tossed it back
And said "you're really a much better suit"
You don't quite know what to say to me
For really, it was you, te brute.

Done

It's not me, Jenn, I promise
I didn't set you up
All I did was pass your name
To the one that held the cup.

And once they saw your work with Muslims
It was they who saw you as true
I was sleeping at the wheel
And didn't know what you'd been through.

Well, it is not my place to say
What the man at Columbia said was right
Jesus made his way to Yale
But in a way you'd find contrite.

There's a lot of responsibility
To being the risen son
"Don't cha know they kill your kin?
And chase you when they're done?"

Judgment

She walked a lonely path
For she'd dare not tell a soul
Involve them in this crazy life
Much better to leave them whole.

She put up with all the judgment
Comments made under the breath
Some even straight to her face
As if she never conquered death.

She let them call her crazy
For little do they know
This game has been going on
Since the very beginning of the show.

Women were once seen as witches[133]
And hung up at the stake
Trying to channel the Holy Spirit
Came to warn about the fake.

But talking in tongues is scary
To those not given the gift
So, they prescribe and prescribe medicine
And never once catch a drift.

Do you know how many Italian moms?
Ended up institutionalized?
They blamed it on the menses
And took them to their demise.

Well to all my gossip kings and queens
To you I say carry on
You'll never admit any wrongdoing
And you'll never be Father John.

---

[133] Erikson, K. (1966). *Wayward Puritans* (p. 67). New York : John Wiley & Sons.

I'll just call you Simons
And let you be as you wish
Put down others to bring you up
Everyone knows that is your dish.

Just one word of caution
Before we enter the afterlife
If you wish to see your loved ones
Put an end to this whole strife.

For if you don't then karma will set in
And suddenly you'll no longer be well
The judgment you place onto others
Will become your very own hell.

The Show

So, I sit and pray in silence
And live my life as a nun
Just hope that someone hears me
Before it's my turn at the gun.

Don't try to communicate
And bring people together for life
Sit and watch in misery
As they twist and turn every strife.

That's the fate I'm dealing with
If anyone cares to know
But don't worry I'll be a good little girl
I won't blow up the show.

From Galilee

He wore porridge in the midnight
And they took down his sword
A mighty tongue with hands that prayed
He touched almost everyone's chord.

But the one that got away
Was the one to chase him down
You can be anti-racist
And still be an evil clown.

You can be top neighbor
And mow your partner's grass
You can lift up your failing spouse
And even wipe her ass.

But if your plotting against the gentle
Is more than I can spare
Your middle will find itself empty
Like the days when you didn't care.

The days when someone called you
And begged you to stop the madness
You silenced your phone
And created a desperate sadness.

And now the day has come
For karma to come through
You need to visit the carpenter
And watch how he comes true.

There is only one person
Who can hold this entity's spirit
He's steady with a hockey stick
And forceful when he steers it.

You need someone with solid trunks
To plant down when he clears it
It has to be a cut above
To hold the devil's spirit.

Select the one whose lesson is strongest
About just what I be
Pick someone who didn't see me
As someone from Galilee.

Her Throne

Friend, I received your poetry
And my, am I impressed
I didn't read it on a platform
But felt it in my chest.

I understand you are a channeler
And can reach out to another world
Where ancestors are clamoring down
Wishing some to end up swirled.

I understand you are a special case
In that you come from quite a "hood"
But what makes you think I did those things?
I would never do anything not good.

I understand you're in the dark
And not sure whom to trust
But let me ask you to evaluate
What happened to your Rust?

Your little friend from childhood
The broken chain that you picked up
You nurtured it as would a mother
A rusty broken chain, the most precious pup.

I don't know too many kids
Who would play cards with their grandfather
I don't know too many kids
Who could root out an imposter.

But may I say I have always known
You were a special breed
The way you write is your tell-all sign
Plus, you went to Al Tawheed.

The Feds were onto you just fine
The minute you walked through that door
The Mosque was already being surveilled
Then in walks good old you, champion of the poor.

They couldn't believe an American girl
Would stand up for their kind
Intrigued by your bravery
They followed you every time.

You were surely onto them
That's why you'd act so crazy
One shoe off and one shoe on
Can shake even the most lazy.

But you conquered them by listening
And they couldn't figure you out
They wanted to save and marry you
Keep you protected during the drought.

You only wanted to understand
And document their most chilling story
But your professors at Yale went astray
And felt you could end in glory.

How do you expect me to believe this line?
When you never came to visit?
How do you expect me to trust in you?
When what you've done is so illicit?

All I can ask is for you to think
About just how much you have grown
You can take care of any crisis
And you never "bitch and moan."

You were not as strong as I
I needed to thicken your skin
But now that I look back on it
I can see it was all in sin.

I was quietly afraid of you
And how compellingly you write
You brought out feelings in me
I only think about in the night.

And now I see how much I've done
To cause your perilous crisis
All I can say from this day
Is wait until they figure out Isis.

I have always known who you were
From the very day that we met
But I had to put you through that test
The test of every Vet.

This way you could understand
Just what it means to truly be alone
This way you'll never leave your kin
Like your loved one who sits on her throne.

Your Sign

You have your health
But you know not your place
You have your wealth
But you're my biggest disgrace.

You left a young girl
Who worshipped your word
You made her suicidal
And bragged when you heard.

You saw innocence
And blamed her God
You hated her optimism
And used your rod.

You are alone now
And Jenny is fine
But you don't belong here
You're not one of my kind.

So, if I could advise you
I'd say hit the pine
Cause your days are numbered
Just like your sign.

Catholic Mass

In this day and age
Some family members look for a check
It could be from the government
It could be from a wreck.

The basic idea of working
Is what makes some want to freak
They rather sit with $800 a month
Than inconvenience the week.

They rather collect disability
For a physical or mental cause
Even if it's trumped up
Like the mother and her gauze.

And in the process of struggling
Survival is all they see
They will knock a baby out of a carriage
And sue her for their knee.

I'm not anti-poor folks
As I am still in the boat
But I will call you out
And watch the lie leave your throat.

I will fix your little behind
If your ways are wicked
I will place your deeds on blast
And watch as you try to trick it.

But at the end of the day
I will give you a pass
For your skills are underrated
Like the words at Catholic mass.

Oh Brother

Your club was afraid of rappers
You met in 1994
You were informed of the violence
You were informed of the floor.

You used geographical distance
And territorial complaint
You set your sights on big names
While your persona was one of saint.

You knew of their deep weakness
They fight amongst each other
It's the saddle of poverty
Italians also do in their own brother.

But the one for you to discover
Is one like no other
He looks for those who could recover
And finds a way to have them smothered.

Oh brother.

This Brawl

I will guide your steps
If you only allow me a chance
I wish to write you some screenplays
That will help you win this dance.

Some will be on my neighborhood
Some will be on the mob
Some will be on how to organize
Without them seeing you sob.

I know I can make an impact
But they will surely create a fall
They do not wish me to reach you
The do not wish me to call.

Like the great ones of the 1960s
They wish most to see me dead
But only after they consume my body
Thinking it will grow their head.

That's why I don't like the hospital
That's why I don't like the ball
Just keep me in sights at all times
And help me beat this brawl.

My Crook

Settle down, Jenny girl
You're going way too fast
You're going to lose some along the way
But the ones who stay will last.

You're trying to unite a bunch
That only cares what's for dinner
Yet, you still try with your compassionate eye
To find the lonely winner.

In your haste, my young granddaughter
You're forgetting that I can help
I know I'm dead but I'm in your head
Just like my old-trade mark welp.

Find a way to publish
And make some money from a book
It's not selfish to feed your family
Plus, you made them look.

I know you're shook
But you're not alone on the hook
I'm here with you as always
I won't let them take my crook.

Shroud of Turin

So, tell me, Mr. Skip and son
Yes, I'm taking your degree away
You think you are the son of God
And orchestrated my final day.

Well, last I checked in all your works
You never thanked your mountain-faced man
All you did was assume his crown
And formulate your sick plan.

You told your friends you were Jesus Christ
And they gave you all the power
To start world wars and toy with believers
My God, I see your final hour.

But in my good bye may I ask you a question?
For I'm about to pull your card
Last I checked for you there is no resurrection
Your *face* doesn't look that hard.

You searched your whole entire life for the son of God
So, you could kill him and assume his role
Well, let me put it to you loud and clear
You're nothing but a big "ash" hole.

You looked for certain facial features
And bone-chips in an array
All the while claiming not to believe
So, you could get them off your display.

Well, one thing you can't take away
Is this right here claim
The true face on the Shroud of Turin[134]
Is my grandfather and he wanted no fame.

---

[134] Craig, E. A., & Bresee, R. R. (1994). Image formation and the Shroud of Turin. *Journal of Imaging Science and Technology, 38*(1), 59-67.

The One

Listen up now, Mr. Skipper
This is Grampa Charles
You mighta had your way with me
But Jenny put you on, like Carl's.

She saw that Jean was out of line
And tested him by removing her cross
That is how the angels came through the door
And showed you just who was boss.

I know you thought you were the man above
Until Jenny wrote you that passage
You knew she came from a crystal ball
And that's how your anger sandwiched.

One is ready to take this on
And I would give him a chance
But the one who should have a talk with you
Is Joe – he's "good with his hands."

To Show

Well, let me remark on your progress
You've taken out half my family
Some to mental illness
Some to made up candy.

But here I am still standing
And you can't break my tree
Another thing you can't change
Is my make-up, your biggest envy.

I am one percent your kind
Which means I fit the bill
But I am also one percent Black
How does that complicate your shrill?

I'm three percent Hispanic
A greater percent Italian
Once converted to Islam
Even pranced in on a stallion

So, tell me what does your *one-drop rule* make me?[135]
A Black Jewish Italian Hispanic Muslim Chick?
Who's Catholic through and through
And that's what makes you sick.

You couldn't create me more divided
And yet my parts all work together
You're the only odd man out
So, you go back and change the weather.

Well, honestly you do not anger me
I've known about you for years
All I needed to know is
Were you involved out of fears?

---

[135] Sweet, F. W. (2005). *Legal History of the Color Line: The Rise and Triumph of the One-Drop Rule*. Backintyme. See also Hickman, C. B. (1996). The devil and the one drop rule: Racial categories, African Americans, and the US census. *Michigan Law Review*, 95, 1161.

Or was it out of necessity?
Because you also believed in the vision?
Did you invite me into Yale?
To make me part of its prison?

Or did you think that possibly?
I could throw you all a line?
You're petty in your academics
And horrible to Dr. Louis Fine.

But somewhere in the journey
I got a soft spot for your game
Perhaps it comes from outwitting you
And bringing you to your shame.

You couldn't stop a Marion girl
If you wavered all your dough
I do not play for money
I'm just waiting for my people to show.

Cape Cod

You haven't sought out history
And for that, you are caught off guard
But Isa is here to give it to you
So, you can run your squad.

Don't let them divide your pod
Stay humble and think of God
You need to be nimble to beat their rod
Lest you end up bitter like Mr. Cape Cod.

Same Old Song

They go to Church weekly
And believe they have an edge
They sacrifice their body parts
Like a martyr and her wedge.

They judge mental illness
Instead of seeing it as trauma
They drink themselves silly
Just so they don't have to think of mama.

They make fun of us for helping
And say we're way too kind
Though they vote democratically
Rarely are they confined.

They use language like enabler
That's what they learn from their plan
Though they pretend to be Catholic
They don't even know Grandpa Stan.

Well, I've been onto you, Virginia
I will not call you by name
All I will simply relay
Is that you know nothing of this game.

You can play along on the news
You can cast some down as evil
But place you in my hood one night
You'd be escaping like Knievel.

Hypocrites never show
When it comes their time to admit
All they simply do
Is claim it was their pit.

Well, if your pit is faulty
Let me suggest some ways
You can make it up to the right one
But you have to lose your downward gaze.

Begin by saying "I'm sorry"
I've judged you as someone wrong
But waiting for them to say it
Is like playing the same old song.

Belong

And now the anger surpasses me
So that I can carry on
It isn't an easy burden to bear
But at least I can trust in John.

There will come a day when you understand
Why I took to writing
There will come a day when you will see
His Majesty in all your sighting.

My voice is to prepare you for
What you already have in your heart
It is not the time for division now
It is time for a brand-new start.

There was a time when we worked
To spend time with our family
Now we're rushing in a race
And can't hear Grandpa Stanley.

I was there the day he passed
When his son could not hold his "worm"
His son squeezed my hand so darn tight
I felt Grandpa Stanley's "Germ."

He looked at me with the most innocent eyes
What he said broke my heart
"You came" is what he exclaimed
Before he let go of his part.

I can't explain it all to you
For you know that eyes are watching
All I can say is settle down
Before you see something shocking.

Jesus will not present himself
Until you clean up this mess
He left very careful instructions
That you still refuse to address.

I'm not saying he's a sandal man
For certainly times have changed
All I'm saying is he protected the weak
While you all walk estranged.

Pick up your boots and backs, my dears
And hum as you play along
We are being watched from afar
And might as well sing us a song.

This way we can communicate
There won't be anything wrong
The times are crouching up on us, Lord
And I need to know where I belong.

Bound

And when it was all said and done
Mohamed, he was correct
The original bible is not in our hands
And that is what I suspect.

But what he does not know
Is that one day religious people will be called to count
Will you follow the written word?
Or one who walks among you, bound?

The Picture

So now that it has left the bag
Tell me, what shall we do?
How can I be the messenger?
If everyone listens to you?

How can I reach a crowd of nine?
And beg them to turn around?
For the way they're living in this world
Makes Footprints weep and frown.[136]

How could I write my heart to folks?
And let them recall a shroud?
For it was two thousand years ago
Who'd remember, who'd even bow?

Well, I won't stir up trouble, Skip
I'll let them live their dreams
Purchasing their way to happiness
While falling apart at the seams.

But in the end the entire trip?
Would it all be in vain?
For who would listen to a white girl now?
The picture is the one they blame.

---

[136] Hart, R. (2019). *Footprints in the Sand*. Retrieved from https://www.ryanhart.org/footprints-in-the-sand/

The Scum

Shout out to Erving Goffman
For setting the record straight
He studied asylums and found
The inmates were the ones who rate.[137]

The people working there
Were crazier than crazy could be
All a bunch of control freaks
Gasping to find the C.

And once they find their C
Tell me, what do they do next?
Sometimes they just torture her
Sometimes they put her to death.

Sometimes they make a call uptown
You know, to outter space
They see if there's any room up there
To hold the one who just might place.

Place as a contender
Here to warn the people
About kings and artificial intelligence
Trying to do away with the steeple.

Jealous of the mystery of faith
And religions of every brand
They have not one clue in their brains
About how we came to stand.

So, search for the Holy C man
Search and search you may
But you ain't never caught a rebel
He still walks among us, pray.

---

[137] Goffman, E. (1961). *Asylums: Essays on the Social Situation of Mental Patients and Other Inmates*. Anchor Books.

As for me I carry his memory
And keep it close to my heart
I wake up each and everyday
Thinking how to best play my part.

My part is of Cassandra[138]
Here to warn you all of danger
Taking your frustrations out on poor white folks
Will not resolve your anger.

Some want to see Italians suffer
Some want to see Italians hum
They think this will settle the score
They plan to celebrate with some rum.

Happy to eliminate the "scum"
Bring your family a death plant like a mum
Say you should have never come
And now you must go back to being a bum.

---

[138] Encyclopedia Brittanic (2023). *Cassandra*. Retrieved from https://www.britannica.com/topic/Cassandra-Greek-mythology.

Pageantry Faith

Ye of pageantry faith
You go to Church on the regular
But when it comes to a true moral crisis
You're silent as black and white memorabilia.

For that, you save some face in public
But with God, you lose your turn
You're only Catholic at mass time
But like Ash Wednesday you will burn.

Chained

They chained her arms to a table
They ordered her to write Greek tragedies
All because she was gifted with charm
They knew she'd predict all calamities.

But out of the corner of the thick Rocky trees
Is a man who holds our destined seas
He walks as strong as Hercules
And he scares all of our enemies.

Socrates.

Off the Wall

She broke down after many years
It was her time to rest
The good Lord couldn't put her at ease
For she was facing a test.

How could she justify all those years?
Of traveling all over the world?
As she left her little girls with a strict man?
Who crumbled at the sight of her curled?

She tried to fight him with her words
But she couldn't quite get it to work
Her brain was a mush of academic jargon
Mixed with meanness from the jerk.

So, she fought and fought but with every move
There'd be some self-sabotage
The woman could not accept what she did
Guilt became her entourage.

Filing lawsuits, calling state agencies
Can't someone out their help?
"I'm a victim of domestic violence"
She'd say and watch the expressive welp.

No one cared for all they saw
Was a paranoid lunatic
But if you want to know what set her off
It was really one swift kick.

The man he doesn't deny this
He defends it with all he can
For she came home late one day and
That didn't sit well with the plan.

But gullible people believe in him
They see him as intellectually prime
If only they saw through little girls' eyes
All he's done to hurt their climb.

They're innocent children for Heaven's sake
They don't belong in a monster's ball
But tell that to Simon Says people
It's like watching paint drip off the wall.

Forgiveness

Forgiveness is a fickle word
Not the kind you'd want to greet
For in that land of "giveness"
Is usually a tie that you must meet.

For me I ask for assistance
And help to get me through
For I know my Lord is busy
And never pray unless I'm true.

For those who pray for Cadillacs
And clothing to make you grand
Consider how busy is our Lord
Protecting us and our land.

But you overload the airways
With your frivolous wish for toys
Never thinking about the soldier
Never asking about the boys.

You think we are so different
And not part of your tribe
Because we care about loved ones
And not the one who takes the bribe.

Well, I guess I won't be seeing you
You never change your ways
Keep thinking this is about race
And I'll watch you count your days.

But if you ever pick up a religious piece
I'll tell you where you'd be
Right back in your train of thought
Cause some folks can never see.

As for me and this forgiveness
I'll tell you what I'll do
If four is the magic number
Make someone's wish come true.

Though there isn't a mortal in this place
Who can claim "I do not forgive"
It is not your place, dear mortal
Please watch your words when you twist.

Forgiveness is up to God, the Lord
And never up to you
So, get up off your high horse, Virginia
And stop this race war too.

The King and I

It was his day to shine
This man from a higher town
He felt it was enough
It was his turn to tear down.

He didn't expect a white girl
To come into his place
Work harder than all the rest
As if there was no such thing as race.

His wife wanted him to be famous
Although he had Christian ideals
He also wanted the fortune
Deep inside he couldn't fight the feels.

So, what was this man's venture?
Tell me, just what did he do?
He went on a TV competition
And became a winner too.

But in his course of climbing
The man forgot his code
You never leave a mate in distress
As you indulge in apple pie a la mode.

But one day when we're long passed this
And effervescent swings
The man might recall the very day
An angel gave him his wings.

And if on that day he remembers
And vows to break code no more
I imagine God will have mercy on him
For truly, he was never poor.

But that white girl who fought so much
To help you build your tree
She might be your only chance
Of making it over to thee.

So, if I were you, I'd listen
And take it all straight to heart
For you never know when it's your last day
To play the king and I, your favorite part.

Two Thousand Years

For two thousand years
You've been plotting the return
Would Jesus come back to save?
Or would Jesus come back to burn?

What would happen on Judgment Day?
Would Jesus punish those who made him stay?
Stay on the cross, you slow-ass fools
Stay on the cross, as their spit met his drools.

Would Jesus free the prisoners?
Would Jesus free the slaves?
Would Jesus tell the Pope?
To sit down and learn to praise?

Would Jesus fear the Muslims?
Or would Jesus see it through?
For they followed his every word
How could they not be true?

Would Jesus do away with riches?
Would Jesus condemn fame?
Would Jesus consider technology?
A threat to us all the same?

Would Jesus cast down mortals?
For committing genocide?
Would Jesus create pandemics?
To keep us all inside?

Would Jesus make you contemplate?
And reflect on all your life?
So that when the day cometh?
You will not be taken by strife?

Would Jesus try to warn you?
That all ain't on the up and up?
Would Jesus try to get you?
To huddle close and hold your pup?

Would Jesus tell you straight out?
This is about World War II?
How America was too late to help?
And let the people suffer the coup?

Would Jesus blow up the one percent?
And spread their wealth to the poor?
Or would Jesus take one look at this world?
And head straight for the door?

For I can't think of a more messed up place
Than the one you all have made
You are not even grateful
For the sun, the moon, or shade.

So, in that sense I understand
Jesus is a threat to this here game
But if it's ok with you all
He came back just the same.

Not really sure just what to do
For now, it's really bad
The situation is exponential
And politicians run us, sad.

Our Jesus

Pontius Pilot had it wrong
Leave it up to the people?
Hell no, they're all evil!
They've been scorned by the steeple.

They wanted to be Jesus
But they just could not
So, when given a chance
They made our Jesus rot.

Pilot should have known better
Than to leave such a plan
Up to everyday people
Up to everyday man.

Everyday man is jealous
Beyond all repair
He can't see passed his nose
He can't see passed his snare.

So let that lesson bear
On events of the day
Why let jealous people?
Wash us all away?

Why do we sit down?
And be lectured upon as rude?
For defending our religion
They treat us oh so crude.

Democracy is in trouble
I am here to say
There is none, so it seems
But there is a better way.

Pick out the noblest of you
From each and every group
Form a diverse alliance
To judge the entire croup.

Don't let them ever divide you
Disciples of the now
Show them who is boss
With a swing and a bow.

Don't let them twist you
On each and every word
Don't let them discount you
Like the mocking bird.[139]

Saddle up for this test
For it's a close as close can be
And fight once and for all
Avenge ol' Galilee.

---

[139] Lee, H. (2010). *To Kill a Mockingbird*. Random House.

I Care

I wish I could have held your hand
And helped you with your cross
I might not have been the strongest one
But I would have worked hard like a boss.

I could have picked up your limbs
When they tired up that hill
I could have wiped sweat from your brow
And held you tight when you were still.

I know it was your sacrifice
And not one anyone else could bear
But I wish I could have walked with you
To show how much I care.

Yale Graduation

I had a hard time in school at Yale
I couldn't find my groove
I kept wanting to apply what I learned
To eradicate poverty and make a move.

I almost didn't submit my dissertation
I let it sit idly for years
I could not make sense of
How to make up for all their tears.

I didn't want to take the pain of Muslims
And let it help my career
I couldn't bear benefiting on account of
What the bad man aimed and steered.

But finally, a professor encouraged me to submit
And when I did, I felt a weight lifted off
I could now use my writing
To try to persuade the loft.

I dreamed of graduation
I wanted Skip to meet Grampa
But he said he wasn't going
And I lost all my stamina.

I never did walk for my PhD
Grampa didn't get to see my cap
But I can still get my story out
You can hear it in my rap.

My Grandfather

You took my grandfather away
I'm talking to you, Mr. Runner
You think you got the heart of "the one?"
Let's see you dazzle us with your stunner.

You took my grandfather away
Number 44 and some counting
Paid the State to send in Jean
Better watch out for your surroundings.

You took my grandfather away
And you think you're all set
Best take your ass to Atlantic City
And see how much you can bet.

You took my grandfather away
And I have caught your burial
Can't say it will be Presidential
But I'll allow your voice to play on stereo.

You took my grandfather away.

Silent Game

They've played a silent game
For many, many, many years
You all wait patiently for Jesus to return
While they chase the poor out of fears.

They've played a silent game
True Catholics believe in reincarnation
They knew the one could be among us
Catholics understand all about devastation.

They've played a silent game
They tried to erase your faith
Never knowing I would come to intervene
I won't let them take you on March 8th.

They've played a silent game.

Humiliation

Humiliation leads to anger
That is what *The Iceman*[140] shows
In his documentary about JC upbringing
He tells you how the rage flows.

Humiliation leads to anger
And it finds a way to get released
Usually onto an innocent one
And not the one who teased.

Humiliation leads to anger
And we do nothing to stop it
Let children be pushed to suicide[141]
While Elon builds a new rocket.

Humiliation leads to anger
And children are always prime targets
Go into schools to train against it
And see how far the bar gets.

Humiliation leads to anger
And Byzantine Catholics know much about this
They dip croutons into vinegar
To remind you what they fed Jesus.

Humiliation leads to anger
But I wonder who bears the blame?
The one who expresses rage and anger?
Or the ones who first put him to shame?

Humiliation leads to anger
From whence does the bitter spew come
It had to come from the original instigator
To his word you must never succumb.

Humiliation leads to anger.

---

[140] Vromen, A. (Director). (2012). *The Iceman* [Film]. Millenium Entertainment.
[141] Cohen, B., & Shenk, J (Director). (2016). *Audrey & Diasy* [Film]. Netflix.

Count Me Out

You thought you'd count me out
Sifted through all my limbers
Never knowing God was watching
Your own father wants you in timbers.

You thought you'd count me out
Framed me since I was an infant
Chose to praise my sister
And accused me of being "distant."

You thought you'd count me out
My candle burns from within me
Swallowed up your sick inferno
And spit it back at you eternally.

You thought you'd count me out
Scheming to take over my power
Never knowing when my luck might run out
And I'll meet my final hour.

You thought you'd count me out
Was dealt a very hard hand
But with Grampa as my Jesus
To the devil incarnate I'll take that stand.

You thought you'd count me out.

Woke Up

I woke up from not sleeping
And found I had forgotten a friend
Got so caught up in the mundane
Didn't realize you felt near the end.

I woke up from not sleeping
And found you on the floor
I knew I had to rescue you
Your spirit had become too poor.

I woke up from not sleeping
Only to learn what I've known all along
My family has not always had my back
They stopped me from singing my song.

I woke up from not sleeping
And I'm asking you for a light
I don't smoke cigars and cigarettes
But my battery isn't running right.

I woke up from not sleeping
And now I have new purpose
Stop thinking of my worries
And help the one crumbling at the surface.

I woke up from not sleeping
And I feel tremendous peace
I know what I've got to do now
I'm surrounded by God's fleece.

I woke up from not sleeping
It's something I highly recommend
Get yourself some cold water
And splash your face until you comprehend.

I woke up from not sleeping.

Dim

I was a graduate student at Yale
And wrote a paper that made him shudder
He called his little cronies
And tried to take me to my slumber.

He invited me to his apartment
Down in the L.E.S.
A friend was onto him
But I still went to his address.

He asked me to read his book out loud
And said it was standard procedure
I was in need of the dough at the time
So, 15 an hour could help my fever.

I was his TA for a while
He'd say "yes, I did get a hare cut"
Laughed to himself about it
But one student called his bluff.

I had a student named "Jihad"
I wonder what happened to him
This Professor was partly responsible
For making my life so dim.

Repent

My friend, why have you forsaken me?
I've shown you nothing but respect
But you wrote books about the ghetto
Without crediting Italian influence.

You only care about your own tent
While whites organize to help you vent
You never credit ethnographers, Heaven-sent
The ones who preceded you, now repent.

Door Knobs

It's not easy to channel the word of God
When you have to work three jobs
You think we have made progress?
We're still a bunch of working-class slobs!

We depend on them door knobs
But they turn into firing squads
They want to see us sob
That's why they belong to Rob.

Move

The joke was on me
Everyone at Yale knew
They scoped me as the maker
Found out I was one percent Jew.

Man, what kind of a screw?
Does it take for you to prove?
That religious people know the truth
It's now time to make your move.

Lady and the Tramp

You cannot outwit me
I am wit personified
I am here to remind you
About the one crucified.

I care about my pride
Just want you all to catch your stride
Try not to fuss and fight
With your own you need my light.

I can settle all the arguments
I can settle all the pain
I was here for many years
But they always declare me insane.

I can't condone this life
You created a world of strife
I can barely even survive
It's deeper than a very cutting knife.

Isa went through it all with you
Genocide, slavery, and the camps
Even got a perpetual stomach bug
From what happened with the lamps.

But like the used towel that's damp
You curse me with your vamp
Never listening to me stamp
It's the story of Lady and the Tramp.[142]

---

[142] Geronimi, C., Jackson, W., & Luske, H. (Directors). (1955). *Lady and the Tramp* [Film]. Walt Disney Productions.

Sucky

Betrayal is a word I've met
Too often for me to note
I met him once when I was down
He wouldn't offer me his coat.

He sent me on a boat
Paid men to slit my throat
But when they saw me, they choked
So, he sent their families home to roast.

You think I'm about bunnies and duckies?
I'm on a mission to get Buckie's
Cause dude was jealous of me so lucky
Until I showed his true self as sucky.

Maimed

My arms shake when I'm channeling
My heart breaks from the pain
But when you see me on the street
You look at me with disdain.

Never knowing I came to exclaim
All that is good about the world we shame
Why guilt people with such blame?
Instead of letting them attest and proclaim?

Jesus was here for you to name
But your religious elites didn't want him in fame
They wanted him to die all the same
And leave him with his heart all maimed.

My Cross

I have been at work meetings
Where my cross was present
I always wear ashes on my forehead
To mark the start of Lent.

But wherever I go people vent
They don't wish Catholics to express our scent
They wish only to charge us high rent
And never once do they ever repent.

I have been ordered by a certain Professor
To remove my cross for a big meeting
"That thing on your neck" must go
Or the audience will never accept your greeting.

You represent the college!
And a cross is not what "we" believe in
So please remove it before you go on stage
We need to keep on with the deceivin.'

Needless to say, I didn't remove my cross
Then the man refused my tenure letter
Set me up not to publish
And I lost my job to the damn debtor.

But around the corner was something better
Now, I'm in position to change the weather
Just need someone who is strong like leather
To help share what came of my feather.

Insane

You need not fight his honor
You need only destroy his name
He sent in men to kill me
So, he could secure his fame.

But you all can play his game
He'll remark that you carry blame
He'll ask you to refrain
From helping those deemed insane.

But, hey, why complain?

Chicken

Harvard vs Yale
That's a game they play real well
Too bad they didn't realize
I'm not the kind to sell.

I'm the kind who rings the bell
Warns you about the dangers of the well
Sees if you can tell
Which one to send to hell.

It's a game of crazy politics
A game that'll make your insides sicken
The game they play is called "hunting Jesus"
It's a high-class game, but I call chicken.

Steam

My biological father named me Jennifer
My mom gave me the middle name "Lee"
When I got older, I prayed for justice
And took the confirmation name Justine.

Now beyond the river's dream
Is a party for Kareem
Their demon will come apart at the seems
Just confront her and watch her steam.

Channel the Fray

You thought you'd take my grandfather
You thought you'd make him pay
You thought you'd make him suffer
You thought you'd change the day.

But out the left side of your beret
I caught the Church's hey
You tried to swipe it from the Christmas display
So, you could take over my way.

Well, Mr. Tttttttipton will never get his say
Cause I pulled the wheels from his tray
Stationary will be his next "lay"
And that's how you channel the fray.

Gin Rummy

Some think we are so foolish
For creating the Easter bunny
You wouldn't if you knew the real reason
I know you all think it's to be funny.

But it's really not about the honey
It's to warn you that they look for "Sonny"
They search for "colored eggs" for their tummy
To see which one is Jesus, you dummy!

They search through eggs of every color
To find the one who could recover
Teach lessons about how to smother
The bad elements in your slumber.

But you're so used to following numbers
You forgot the story of the first comers
Jealousy took over their summers
While true believers took to hummers.

And like the Easter bunny
I'll be sitting here with no money
Waiting for you big dummies
To realize I'm gin rummy.

Sweet

She fell asleep on the cold floor
It was a mighty feat
To travel from Heaven to Earth
And then get knocked down by defeat.

But it was cool to watch everyone retreat
Try to pull lessons from the washing of the feet
When the whole entire journey was about Pete
And what he did to prevent our meet.

Yeah, he's real sweet.

Vampire

It took five officers to settle me down
My heart was burning on fire
To see how respected the bad man is
I'm taking about the one wishing to retire.

He thinks he's the Messaiah
But deep inside he has too much desire
He won't acknowledge me as sire
Rather see me go down as liar.

The true vampire.

Your Reign

The day is dawning down on us
Though the air is fairly crisp
I'm wondering if you'll show yourself
Or is it too much for you to risk?

I know your folly carefully
I've grown it from the vein
It's there to help you get through life
But all I hear is you all complain.

You think you are so sane
But in the afterlife you'll be fighting pain
Never able to stop a plane
Because you went after my hair of grain.

Enjoy your reign.

INRI

I'm nailed right in
You didn't get the memo?
Oh, my bad they only send it to their own
So, you could forget the demo.

But on the day you refill your ammo
I'll be sitting low like Sammo
Waiting for you to tap Rambo
See if he can avenge the Tambo.

Damn, yo!

Kin

Sentimental ties to place
Is where my heart begins
It doesn't mean I haven't room for you
It means you have some sins.

And before the bad man wins
I'm begging you to help your kin
Lest you end up in hell with your fin
On account of what you did to Gin.

True Slayer

100 years ago you were born
And my, am I impressed
Little one come back to life
To fix what the bad man messed.

He didn't have a sailor suit
When he met my nonna
It was at a five and dime store
He was home from the war, a loner.

He admired Nonna's arms
And how she looked in a sweater
Thought those arms could hold some children
And the days seemed to look better.

He didn't know he was noticed
By the bad man in the Navy
He thought he escaped their snare
But they took it out on Mavie.

Mavie brought the gifts he had
And wowed the entire floor
He didn't know they were using him
They cracked open the ceiling door.

But when you are poor
Those who help seem like a savior
It's difficult to discern true motive
When your tummy rumbles out of misbehavior.

You think your group isn't favored?
God gave you all his flavor
But you didn't realize it was to make you braver
So, you could fight against the betrayer.

A true slayer.

Him

The day is starting slowly
I can barely feel my limbs
Exhausted from the struggle
My mind sees miss thing Sims.

But at the corner of the rim
As LeBron begins his trim
You will find the light to dim
Before our world goes to him.

Ironic Fact

It is a little-known ironic fact that those who are most in need of help are least likely to ask for it.

Family:

A group of people who are supposed to care
Family

Lint

You started makin' money
You thought you had an edge
All your cars and houses
Were they Heaven-sent?

No, you ripped off Indians during Lent
Sold them cars that couldn't vent
Laughing as they tried to pay the rent
While you purchased your grand tent.

You left the Catholics in your family bent
Never bothered to make a dent
You thought your riches made gave you cents
But in reality, your soul is spent.

I'm sending you to hell for your next stint
You ignored my pleas with your tint
You figured your way of life was mint
But all you are is extra fuzz like lint.

Luce

Some of my fellow Christians
I'm sorry to break the bad news
But you've been following the one
Who tried to steal it from the pews.

He wants my head up in a noose
So, no one can threaten his goose
He thinks he's the risen Juice
When he's really just a big caboose.

Yo Ace, you're following "Luce."

Embrace

Sigh lent Peter, have you heard me?
I know you have some faith
It might not come out in your academic work
But I can see it in your face.

Unlike the very delicate lace
I've come here to help you place
Don't fall for the devil talk about race
Live your life as did the most amazing grace.

It's time to embrace.

Possum

Now your insides are all sweaty
Unsure if you're part of the problem
Let me put it to you swiftly
Your "knot's" in a borrowed costume.

He's scheming and he's plotting
About how he can beat the Cherry Blossom
But I can see right through his wicked bottom
Still, you glorify him as he plays possum.

Go stop him!

Honey Dew

Upon your final hour
I will not be there for you
You crept into my power
And left me dry on cue.

You pretend you are so true
But unlike the mighty honey dew
Your message is neither sweet nor green in hue
It's sour just like your wicked voodoo.

Man, you are a screw.

High Class

I was an unplanned segment
Never was supposed to last
They kicked me to the gutter
But I rose like a Navy ship's mast.

Still, he tried to nab me fast
Doesn't want me to bring up the past
Just keeps focusing on his sash
So, he can be crowned king of ash.

Somebody holds my stash
Mr. Houston is a blast
Encouraged you to think selfishly like a caste
And end ties with Catholic mass.

I never gave him my pass!
But he read my poem through the glass
Published it as a book with all my sass
While you all roll around in your own trash.

Yeah, he's real high class.

Candlestick Maker

He divided his belongings
Gave them to perfect strangers
Little Marc got his harmonica
I received his shirts and dangers.

But it was the man with all the anger
Who followed the one from the manger
Let him live weighed down like a heavy anchor
Cause deep inside he's sorer than a canker.

Still the dude's a polite thanker
Left me run over by a tanker
He's trying to fill the role of banker
But that position belongs with me
The true candlestick maker.[143]

For Heaven Sakes, er.

---

[143] Forsyth, H. (2016). *Butcher, Baker, Candlestick Maker: Surviving the Great Fire of London.* Bloomsbury Publishing.

Katyn Massacre

It was around the Katyn Massacre
The Holy Spirit was flying to the people
They were told God would meet them
And she represented the steeple.

But out of the damn peep hole
Came the man whose car was repo'd
Said "it's not your turn" like a creep would
Stabbed her in the back as only he could.

Some Europeans were left to freeze and
They started fearing the breeze and
They stopped all from believin' and
Started reppin' for the demon.

Always schemin.'

My Tradition

Friday will mark your 100th birthday
And it couldn't be more fitting
April 7th falls on Good Friday this 2023 year
At Church will be some ladies sitting.

As for me, I'll be reminiscin'
About how you lived better than a Christian
Never concerned about material schism
Cheering up the broken was your mission.

The pass was made and I'm in position
But I need some help with my volition
I'm just a mom not a full magician
But you could learn from my tradition.

This Life

He disassembled his chair
The day after he died
Donated his clothes to the rehab
As I was dying inside.

He divided up some items
Gave them to the club
As I stayed watching his gestures
Was it Judas back at the rub?

I warned my whole entire family
But no one believed my word
The one acting oh so innocently
Is the one who made Grampa hurt.

But you stay steadily waiting
For a man to come from the sky
I'll sit here already knowing
He was here in this life.

Aboriginal

He was like an aboriginal
Walked among animals as one
Hands were worn from years of work
But his smile was bright like the sun.

He was like an aboriginal
A medic in the war by nature
Could heal a sickened heart
Remove how much he hates ya.

He was like an aboriginal
And I am his granddaughter
Learned many lessons from him
About how to avoid slaughter.

He was like an aboriginal.

Torcher

Set the table for a real nice dinner
Make sure your knick-knacks are in order
Then pour your favorite glass of wine
And wear a t-shirt showing you're a supporter.

But in due time, you all will falter
For you never see me as coming from the altar
Send money to foreign lands to escape torture
While your own flesh and blood live a scorcher.

You're nothing but a torcher.

Wavy

Your true name is Apollo
And no, I won't forgive your soul
You took the life of Cassandra[144]
And made her lose her role.

Your deal was that she could see the future
But she'd owe you one secret wish
She'd have to declare there is no God
It was God you wanted to diss.

So, Cassandra reneged on the offer
And was immediately deemed crazy
Her curse was no one would ever believe her
Even her grampa who served in the Navy.

Her hair is wavy.

---

[144] Encyclopedia Brittanic (2023). *Cassandra*. Retrieved from https://www.britannica.com/topic/Cassandra-Greek-mythology.

A Miracle in Your Honor

I witnessed a miracle in your honor
It doesn't compare to a flying saucer
But I once rescued an infant
From the craving arms of Gibraltar.

I witnessed a miracle in your honor
It was the gift of reincarnation
Here to provide some hope to those
Living with devastation.

I witnessed a miracle in your honor
You saved me from death many times
I only wish I could show the world
But I can't, so I convey it in my rhymes.

I witnessed a miracle in your honor
I wish you had never gone away
But I still see you now and again
You're an angel to those in disarray.

I witnessed a miracle in your honor.

Revelation's Form

I know I'm not in Revelation's form
But I can still hold your tear
I know you try to slow its roll
But I can always feel it, so dear.

I know I'm not in Revelation's form
But I have never left your side
I've been the one waking you up in life
With me you can never hide.

I know I'm not in Revelation's form
But I haven't changed my name
You can ring me up in your prayers at night
And I'll help you through your blame.

I know I'm not in Revelation's form
But I would like to reach out
I see we're in a moral fight
And wish to help us in this drought.

I know I'm not in Revelation's form
But I'll still sail the ocean blue
I'll build a place you can call home
If you can just keep my word true.

I know I'm not in Revelation's form
But you've never forgotten my light
Just buried a bit beneath your bling
Is Jesus and he wants you to fight.

Down

You didn't see me when I was down
I hid behind my postured smile
You didn't see me when I was down
You passed me on by in that while.

You didn't see me when I was down
Too busy painting your nails
You didn't see me when I was down
You were on a boat enjoying the sails.

You never see me when I am down
I guess it's too hard to take that look
You never see me when I am down
But you can read what you missed in my book.

You never see me when I am down.

Talks with Jesus

I didn't know that many years ago
There'd be a time I would long to see
How many times you held my hand?
How many times you comforted me?

I didn't know the day would come
And I'd have no one to hug
There's no one like my grampa
He came from up above.

I didn't know your voice would play at night
And tell me that "He" really sees us
I didn't know you'd become my Holy Ghost
And I'd fill them in on our talks with Jesus.

In Prison

Charles Joseph was in prison
Looked up to the upper left
Could not believe he landed there
After ridding the world of the undressed.

Charles Joseph was in prison
He threw up every night
Sick to his stomach over evil
While keeping his lip held tight.

Charles Joseph was in prison.

Hillbilly Gold

They included him in a play
Even used his name Charlie Rhodes
My daughter has a part in this play
She asked me to read his role.

But when I saw his name unfold
In print about hillbilly gold[145]
My hurt I could barely control
For, the lengths to which will they go.

I knew of the Jenin camp
Where they wish to strand me
I knew of the game Jenga
Where the tower falls to the enemy.

But I didn't know they also marked Grampa
Right in plain daylight
That's how they like to do it
In your face with a buried playwright.

But beyond the writer's paid fight
Is one who can't be played right
Perhaps you'll join me as I fly the kite
It's that Je ne sais quoi that'll keep you up at night.

---

[145] Le Roma Greth (1952). *Headin' for the Hills: A Hillbilly Play in Three Acts*. Cedar Rapids, IA: The Heuer Publishing Co.

Bloom

If you had to select one person
To begin a "colony" on another planet
Would you select the best of you?
Or would you lose control like Janet?[146]

What if selecting the one you love most?
Would mean you might never again see them?
What if you decided to send our "junk?"
Would that one day be used as grievance?

These are the questions are leaders ask
This is the question of "whom"
But what they don't know is that God is real
He's preparing you to fight this doom.

It is time to bloom.

---

[146] Harris, J., Jackson, J., Lewis, T. (1986) "Control" [Recorded by Janet Jackson] On *Control*.

Humblest Leader

Leaders, you have done some work on us
Our youth is now unprepared
Heaven forbid something should happen to us
They would be forever scared.

They don't know how to fight this force
They've been coddled into personal identity
Can't see themselves as part of the collective
They bow down to environmental eternity.

At this present time
I ask you for a concession
You know you've messed with American minds
That part's not even in question.

But still, I ask you to visit my section
Walk in the steps of the one from the resurrection
Then if you feel the most modest inner direction
You'll know he selected you for our protection.

I ask you now to do me one solid
I ask you to make up for your deed
All you have to do
Is teach youth why we bleed.

Show them how to fight internal greed
Show them how nature provides a seed
Teach them about honor and to balance weed
Become the humblest leader that we need.

My Mouth

My heart is very strong today
Our ancestors are clamoring down
They're asking me to reach out to you
But that you not make a sound.

I know you know they follow me around
I ask that you do your best to help me out
You were gifted with height to make them pout
But right now, you're all like Thomas in doubt.

I know your culture says not to shout
I learned "honor" from my Asian route
Can you help us through this drought?
Top top has come down to their south.

And I have to watch my mouth.

Most Righteous

What are they afraid of?
That's what you want to know?
Jesus would make sure the poor in *every country* is fed
And that's why they don't want him to show.

Though they stay very close in the know
They won't give it to an American ho
Stay searching for hillbilly gold
But they don't realize he can't be sold.

They know each and every soul
Would benefit from words she wrote
But they don't want her people to feel consoled
They want to break religious spirits whole.

For, if the poor have food and clean water
They'd be better positioned to fight us
They could even take over the world!
They could do what we did to them to spite us.

This is their most righteous.

Quad

Now dust off all your Bibles
And study them verses hard
Challenge them to a duel
And pull their final card.

Tell them they're acting odd
Take them on a visit to Cape Cod
Ask them for their "ear pod"
Take them to a cliff so they can meet God.

They messed with the wrong nod
Feed them super sod
Give them their Axelrod
Roll over their body of work with your quad.

Bleed

So, to my fellow Catholics
May I ask where you've been?
I know the clothes at Bloomingdales
Can be tempting just as sin.

I know that keeping up with Jones'
Is something you're trained to do
For you just wish the best for your family
And want them to succeed too.

But somewhere in your slumber
As you set out to forget your pain
You forgot to look for Jesus
In the eyes of GI Jane.[147]

You thought him as a mister
You thought him as a man
You never ever considered
A change of gender plan.

Yentl[148] didn't tip you off
Because you look for laughs
Canarsie didn't warn you
Jonathan Rieder and his cast.[149]

But friends, you didn't realize
The Holy Spirit would come first
To warn about the crises
To warn about the hearse.

You got so stuck on Muslims
Thinking they were here to harm
Never considering at all
That they were also under Jesus' arm.

---

[147] Scott, R. (Director). (1997). *G.I. Jane* [Film]. Buena Vista Pictures.
[148] Streisand, B. (Director). (1983). *Yentl* [Film]. MGM/UA Entertainment.
[149] Rieder, J. Canarsie(1987). *The Jews and Italians of Brooklyn Against Liberalism*. Harvard University Press.

Under the arm of the Prophet
Does it really matter what we say?
Jesus is a child of God
Just like each one of us, now pray.

But what unsettles me at this time
Is your loyal allegiance to a base
A base that works against you
Like the plots of David Chase.

I'm not asking you to kill friendships
I'm not asking you to flee
I'm just asking if you really know
Why some are so close to thee?

It is not for good intentions
It is not to help you succeed
It is rather to shame you out of
Standing for the one who did bleed.

Fight

I get no love from liberals
I talk too much about God
I get no love from conservatives
Too greedy to share the cod.

I'm cast out by Black and Brown
I'm looked down upon by privileged white
But still I came down to see
If you're gonna let them win this fight.

The battle is not mine
For how could I avenge my own?
Wouldn't that be narcissistic?
Like a contender stealing the throne?

I'm not here to ask for pity
I'm not here to hang in a tree
I'm asking if an ounce of you remembers?
What happened in ol' Galilee?

For what I know that went down
Was not right at all, indeed
I know that what went down
Fell further than a seed.

But I won't ask for compassion
I won't ask for a plea
I'll just ask you to remember
What happened to our beloved JC?

And if you can remember?
Or put yourself back in that place?
Would it really matter?
What he wore, what was his race?

Wouldn't it be about?
The kind of life he led?
And how he inspired masses?
By transforming loaves of bread?

I'm not here to preach
I'm no here to depress
I'm just here to remind you
We are in a test.

The test is will you cave in?
And say "sure that's alright?"
When you know deep inside it's not
Will you cowah or will you fight?

A Dime

If any of "yous" are LEOs
And you'd like to check my facts
All you have to do
Is interview the one who cracks.

I'd start with good old Columbia
All the professors through and through
You'd be surprised just who was in on
The good ol' swtich-er-oo,

Interrogate their motives
And remove what you've been told
The phrase "Death to America"
Is bought, but rarely sold.

What is more common than dramatists
Are the ones controlling the strings
You won't find them decked to the nines
Because they think they're kings.

You'll find them in academic journals
And yes, I know it's a snore
But if solid people don't read what they write
You'll be facing a really big boar.

For deep within those articles
Are tips for how they play
Never disregard a hit count
But watch always what they say.

Not shy to be part of it
Rather proudly do they boast
Critique each and every religious piece
And send the authors home to roast.

All this time you've been searching
For answers from the FBI
The FBI ain't with you
Better off with diamonds in the sky.

Local police, I'm talking to you
Like I've never talked before
You can read my records
You can even the score.

But one thing they won't tell you
Are the miracles that they've seen
Those they watch in private
Seeping the whole time, 90 proof steam.

But verily I implore you
To search just one more time
For I think the mantra you've been sold
Has outworn its weight like a dime.

On 911

I lost a friend on 911
It was someone I hold dear
Warned me about devastation
By tugging at my fear.

I lost a friend on 911
It was a firefighter I never met
He still comes to me in my dreams
And I try to replay the set.

I lost a friend on 911
After he saved people from every creed
The day will go down in history
As one that made religious people bleed.

I lost a friend on 911
And he has come into my heart
He won't let me keep this story hidden
He's calling me to tell you this part.

I lost a friend on 911.

Memorial Day

A salute to an officer
I could not let the day pass
To know you have sacrificed your entire life
And your only comfort is your flask.

One hundred pounds of equipment
Carried carefully in your rucksacks
Far away from friends and family
You fight to protect us from attack.

You can't hug and hold your infants
For you've learned painfully how to wait your turn
You work for less than 2,000 a month
And pray the missile won't catch you on the burn.

But some refer to you as wack
Never crediting the graves, they slack
Only considering their own damn back
Never saluting you with their grand plaque.

They think they are so different
They blame you for killing the poor in other countries
Never knowing you've been set up
Some powerful folks put on a front tease.

But before you order your gun freeze
Let me ask you if you know about the blunt trees
Keep you informed about their dunk, C's
Until you scare them with your sudden sneeze.

They leave you on the cold hard cement to freeze
Though you fight against their identified enemies
They don't care to help you with your PTSD
Only wish to scare you into complacency.

Well, I say "wait and see!"

I Stand for the American Flag

I stand for the American flag
Not because I think our country's perfect
But my grandfathers fought for the innocent
And my uncle laid down his kerchief.

I stand for the American flag
Not because we have no problems
But because our brave men and women
Sacrificed their lives to try to solve them.

I stand for the American flag
Not because I am a "racist"
But because I believe in hope
That we can one day come to face it.

I stand for the American flag
Not because I think we're special
But because God gave us opportunity
We're part of his grand mess hall.

I stand for the American flag
Because deep down in the tropics
It appeared to Grampa when he was low
And it helped him beat the shock pit.

I stand for the American flag
Because if we hadn't fought in WWII
Jupiter would have taken over the US
And we'd all bow down to "you."

I stand for the American flag
That is how we honor our soldiers
Would you like to be separated from family?
Never able to lift your child on your shoulders?

I stand for the American flag.

Tell Them

Tell them who I was
I once walked around with pure innocence
Got kicked down to the gutter
Tried climbing up that barbed-wire fence.

Tell them who I was
I used to be very cheerful
Could dance like one's business
Before I grew too tearful.

Tell them who I was
I once fought for all mankind
Tried to get you food and shelter
Hoped you'd remember me in time.

Tell them who I was
I no longer have it in me
Walked a very drunken line
To trick my most wicked enemy.

Tell them who I was
When I'm dead and gone
Tell them I fought for them
Stood up to the dapper don.

Tell them who I was.

All Whites Privileged

It's not nice to call all whites privileged
You don't know a modicum of our pain
We Catholics were taught to hide it
And dance amidst the rain.

It's not nice to call all whites privileged
You don't know where we've been
Centuries of raw emotion
Live deep within us, my friend.

It's not nice to call all whites privileged
It undercuts our whole struggle
We fight with friends and family
To make sure you're safe in the rubble.

It's not nice to call all whites privileged
You have no clue of what happens
Behind closed doors with ambulances
You'd feel gut-wrenching pain in our rappin.'

It's not nice to call all whites privileged
You know nothing of our sacrifice
But I won't say a word about it
I'll let you live your best life.

It's not nice to call all whites privileged
And I know where it comes from
Academics wanting to put white ethnics down
Have told you we are gruesome.

It's not nice to call all whites privileged
But still, I'll walk the walk
Let you talk down to me
So, you could take over Jack's stalk.

It's not nice to call all whites privileged
I've never had a bad word for you
Black, Latinx, LGBTQIA+ always welcome by me
Still, I get kicked out on cue.

Friends, who told you it's ok to call all whites privileged?
What does that say of domestic violence?
To know the excruciating hell some whites face
Have to keep it hushed in silence.

It's not nice to call all whites privileged
Some are treated like sex-slaves
Make women work long, long hours
Clean the house and get locked in a cave.

It's not nice to call all whites privileged.

Thus Bound

Shortly, you will receive a package
Within it will be a book of poems
I ask that you hold onto it
In the event my cover is blown.

I ask that you tell my "loved ones"
You know the ones that follow me around
That even if I die before I publish
My word is still written, thus bound.

My Chair

First take them to a nice place
Show them what they could have
Get 200 luxury items
And make them look super rad!

Tell them all they need to do
If they want these things
Is tell you what they did wrong
Who in their life did they sting?

Watch closely as you walk them through
For they will have very little to share
They do think they are deserving of goods
Even though they have not one ounce of care.

Play a game of truth or dare
Show them tapes of folks they put in despair
Ask them to clear the air
And tell them "it's only fair."

And they'll stare
For never had they had to bear
A burden that is so rare
Then introduce my chair.

Pressure-cooked Water

When you apply the morality test
Recall that you will find two groups
One will say whatever you want
Those are not the ones behind my coups.

Those are the ones been brainwashed
Into thinking things make them matter
Those can be helped along
If you redo the whole pitter-patter.

It will take some work on re-raising them
To get them to learn the lesson
But at least they won't fade like the other
Into a pot of boiling Wesson.

For the second group is far, far worse
They don't even want what you offer
All they want is to shame God
Send him to the slaughter.

He fancies himself as a reporter
But he's nothing but a distorter
Crushed my spirit like pressure-cooked water
And now we can't afford, er.

A Friend

I know the roles in my religion
I know them very well
But we can't win this war
Without reaching over to hell.

We can't sit in luxury
And watch our brave men fall
We can't sleep throughout the night
Knowing one day he will call.

Well, one day is upon us
And I have no one left
Has anyone seen Mohamed?
The one who has a cleft?

I can certainly use him
A true and loyal friend
To help me understand this world
For clearly, I can't pretend.

So, I send
Messages as would a pen
There's a writer at the age of 10
Who wishes you to comprehend.

That we can't easily blend
Pick up our own rear end
And place us on the mend
We need ourselves a friend.

Lethal Weapon

I am Isa the Holy Spirit
I am Jesus your brother
I am God the Father
I am Mary your mother.

But I am currently smothered
From the indifference to one another
I can't seem to recover
What happened to Mel and Danny Glover?[150]

Oh brother,
I'm a lethal weapon like no other
Pretty soon you will seek blubber
To guard against each other.

Your mother
Sits around never to discover
The only one who truly loved her
Was the one that led like a runner.

Your punner.

---

[150] Donner, R. (Director). (1987). *Lethal Weapon* [Film]. Warner Bros.

Your Love

Let's open up and ask
A question often heard
A controversy spread
Through words that seem absurd.

Examine all the facts
And think without your mind
For an answer will arise
Which you need not search to find.

Oh God, please tell me why
You take the good ones first
Why not take the bad?
Are all the good ones cursed?

My daughter was so innocent
A sweet and loving soul
With her smile—all she had
She made your world seem whole.

Yet, you took her from me—why?
What reason could there be?
Why not take a bad person?
And make him pay the fee?

But no, you took my baby
Somewhere far and high above
And now she's gone away
Without her mother's love.

My sweet and loving child
Don't be bitter or feel such vex
For you must know I love you
But love can be complex.

The statement you have made
Is somewhat true, indeed
The good ones do go first
And now my case I'll plead.

I am only one
Yet, Father to you all
You are my sweet children
Whom I can't greet or call.

From time to time I breakdown
And tears may then result
For I too miss my children
And wish we could consult.

Therefore, when I look down
And see your works on land
I can't resist the moment
To reach out and grab your hand.

But when I pull your hands to me
And swing you all around
I get caught up in your laughter
And lift you off the ground.

So, this is how it happens
How the good ones come above
But really, can you blame me?
My weakness is your love.

The Channeler

They wish to kill the channeler
They have me pegged as God
They hear him in my writing
And they see me as rather odd.

I am not the only one
The same has happened to leaders
They wish to stop the unification
Of God's supreme cheerleaders.

What I'd like you all to do
Is become my dissertation readers
So many of the wrong group
Have read it like the son of Peter.

With the information gained
They hold back like a wide receiver
We need our very own quarterback
To carry our soul like a golden retriever.

The Monster

Listen to my voice
I will not steer you wrong
You think you have a choice?
Your parting song is long.

I cannot remove your arm
Or operate as a medical doctor
I can barely hold my own
For you treat me as an imposter.

And I can't seem to prosper
Too many carbs soaked in my pasta
But I can't afford no lobster
So, I give it all to the mobster.

Cut you down and work to stop ya
Cause you're not on my roster
What I need right now is Kevin Costner[151]
Be my bodyguard against the monster.

---

[151] Jackson, M. (Director). (1992). *The Bodyguard* [Film]. Warner Bros.

Trampled

I wish I could tell you he's coming
I wish I could tell you he's here
But all I can seem to tell you
Is there are some things to fear.

The man who exchanged his life
But not in the way you think
He sacrificed his very soul
To help me in a brink.

But you all never learned the lesson
The lesson of never trusting the crowd
Pilot knew better than jealous men
Yet, he still let them scream so loud.

And our brother was taken down
For all the world to see
Pilot decided to shame him
The Prince of Galilee.

You forgot about the Crucifixion
You forgot about the lonely walk
But they have stayed steadily waiting
For the day he returns his stalk.

They fear he will lash out in anger
They fear he will take away their wealth
They fear he will unite the working class
And lead as would the most stealth.

So, they set up plans to try to catch him
Make him feel low like real bad trash
All the while they're collecting
A wad of Christmas cash.

They set up coups to stop him
While you all say "how sad"
Another with mental illness
Let me ridicule what seems bad.

And now that the day is upon us
Man, will you be sorry
You chose to drink and laugh
While they trampled on your party.

Skull and Bones

I have always known who I was
I didn't need to hear your side
I needed you to be a mentor
Someone with whom I could confide.

I didn't need you to tell your friends
I didn't need you to tell your kind
I needed you to help me through
I needed to relieve my mind.

But you saw me as attractive prey
In that I could unite the working class
You saw me as a dangerous threat
You saw me as having too much sass.

I understand you felt my vision
But shuddered at the final thought
You chirped to Skull and Bones
You bragged about what you bought.

And now that your day is ending
May I ask if it was worth your time?
For your next life will be in misery
You're nothing but a piece of slime.

Love Loss

There is no love loss for me
I've traveled a tumultuous road
There is no way to understand it
It's akin to a manic episode.

There is no love loss for me
I've been burned by nearly all my bridges
Worked like a slave since infancy
Never getting any of those three wishes.

There is no love loss for me
I've sheltered in place like a nun
Stood up to the demon
While recreating her son.

There is no love loss for me
I've been through hell and back
Not sure how to tell you
You'll soon be down for the attack.

There is no love loss for me
I once killed the devil
Came back down to earth
To warn you about the peril.

There is no love loss for me
My skin makes me unrelatable
People don't look to my character
They rather see me deflate like an inflatable.

There is no love loss for me
People have wild ideas about what it means to be white
Think we wake up to catered breakfast
When all we wake up to is a new fight.

There is no love loss for me
I wasn't even loved as an infant
Someone decided I ought to be treated like a dog
Deemed poor like those saved by Saint Vincent.

There is no love loss for me.

As a Child

You didn't know me as a child
I could pitch a kickball like no one's business
Do perfect cartwheels down the street
To prove my worth in this fit test.

You didn't know me as a child
I could scare the devil out of his cage
Bring him back to life so you could meet him
Figure out what to put in his place.

You didn't know me as a child
I could cook a real good baked ziti
Make sure your belly is fully before work
Even write you all a brand-new treaty.

You didn't know me as a child
And I kinda wish you did
I'm old and washed up nowadays
Some days it gets hard to live.

You didn't know me as a child
I have become a middle-aged survivor
Fighting with all my strength
To remind you to unseat the conniver.

You didn't know me as a child.

Final Ciao

The proof is in the damage
In case it is not clear
How much did it shake me?
How much did it make me fear?

But in my lonesome struggle
I've managed to make a friend
Someone whose life was empty
Someone to recommend.

Friends and loyal family
I thank you for your ear
I have my confirmation
The coast is very clear.

My chapter on 911
Published by Russell Sage[152]
Is the piece that did me in
The man tossed me in a cage.

He was in charge of order
And placed me at page 133
It was their secret inside code
Their way of marking me.

And now that it's all over
I think I will take my bow
The curtain has been removed
And I bid my final ciao.

---

[152] Bryan, J. (2005). Constructing "the true Islam" in hostile times: The impact of 9/11 on Arab Muslims in Jersey City. *Wounded City: The Social Impact of 911*, 133-162.

Dirty

Called "dirty" as a child
Because of his background
He vowed to get them back
Without making a sound.

He's responsible for world wars
And inner-city frowns
But if you really want to know
I'd say that one is clown's.

Like the film "Inside Out"[153]
His persona is that of disgust
You can gain purity from him
For surely, he does not lust.

But ask him for a favor
And he'll sink into his hole
He prides himself on being useless
To the one who once made him whole.

Rock and roll.

---

[153] Docter, P. (Director). (2015). *Inside Out* [Film]. Walt Disney Studios Motion Pictures.

Rot

It was your comment about religion
The way you humanized your bunch
The way you understood your Muslims
The way you talked about your lunch.

I saw you from a distance
And invited you all the way in
I needed someone to take my place
Someone whose face was thin.

This way all the reporters
Could focus attention on you
I could live my life in peace
And watch them tackle your crew.

I'm not sorry I did it
I do not care about your lot
If I'd known your power sooner
I would have found a way to make you rot.

True Believer

You saw me through your prism
I fit a certain mold
You kept me around out of pity
You needed someone to scold.

But like Biggie and his song "Juicy"[154]
Your judgment only makes this sweeter
"My crew was lame" like "Sky's the limit"[155]
But your ass was first called by Peter.

A true believer.

---

[154] Wallace, C. (1994). Juicy [Recorded by the Notorious B.I.G.] On *Ready to Die* [Album]. Bad Boy, Arista.

[155] Wallace, C., Kent. C., Caldwell, B., Eaves III, H., Williams, J. (1997). Sky's the Limit [Recorded by the Notorious B.I.G.] On *Life After Death* [Album]. Bad Boy, Arista.

Rule Over You

Your channeling is impeccable
For I never uttered those words
If I had my way with you
You'd be left out for the birds.

I know you want to see the best in me
But there really isn't much to share
You Italians laughed at WWII
And you Catholics did not care.

So, now I'll take it out on you
Why not? You're a very good target
I saw what you went through in life
And how you married the son of Margaret.

But that doesn't sway my thought of you
For clearly you care too much
I won't give my heart to you
Or carry you in a clutch.

One thing I will say to you
Is that you played the game really well
But financially I will crush you down
Just like the man who can't seem to sell.

Best hold your tongue when the spirit comes
And pours out all on cue
Remember, I let you into my club
And that's how I rule over you.

Sick

I wrote directly from the heart
And this is what he said
You use the letter "I" a lot
Self-important, he read.

Not that I would use my life
To reach out to somebody
Not that I put my flaws on display
Better off tell nobody.

For many years I stayed stuck
How could I write without I?
He did this purposely to me
So that I wouldn't try.

But look at his re-released book
And all he says is I
Never thinking he'd be caught on hypocrisy
He had diamonds in his eye.

He also said the word "told"
Was a journalist trick
Well, that's my grandfather's word
Which means that man is sick.

I Sigh

And so, you really did it
You did those things I said
My goodness how you planned
The coroners of the dead.

But I read
Your works like a birdie eats worms
I devoured your apathy
And spit you out like germs.

And I confirm you are nothing
But I am woman
You are parody
I look to Grandpa Stan.

But you ran
As did your family
From my hand
You're as hollow as a taco shell
As hard to catch as sand.

Try Iran
If you want
Get you a homeland
For all who didn't fight
But then complained on command.

You're banned
From my religion
And all I stand for
You're like a 60-year-old
At the Jersey shore.

And I'm poor
As they come
Though richer in morals
I'm rarer than a reef
Send you outback with the Corals.

You recoil
Each time you spew your lie
I swallow up your hatred
And spit in your eye.
I sigh.

Grace

My dear and loving daughter
You need not protect a soul
A soul is what brings you from fear
And carries you out from the cold.

A soul can bring you fire
A soul can bring you ice
A soul can teach a little young girl
What's wrong and what is nice.

But when a soul is broken
It takes more than just God's hands
It takes a whole community
To make them join the plans.

It takes an entire village
It takes an entire tree
But one thing it cannot take
Is your ticket to eternity.

I'm not here to sway believers
I'm not here to say "I'm the true"
I'm here to stand in for the sacred
And deliver all of you.

So, put down your petty scissors
And stop dividing yourselves into race
The winner will not only stop the competition
They will teach you a lesson about grace.

One Day

I thank you for your writing
I know it's taken a toll
I'm sorry for all the fighting
I'm sorry for how they roll.

I know you gave me an alibi
And I can claim to be a senile man
But you gave me something I've never had
Friendship without a ban.

I know you want me to claim I don't know you
So, I can whisk away at your sight
But I'm a lot stronger than you can believe
I was born to take on this fight.

I know you needed a mentor
Someone white-haired like Grampa was
But no one can replace that man
He gives us a permanent buzz.

I will stick with you in your dying days
As I can only imagine you meant well
I just need you to answer one question
Is what you're living in Heaven or Hell?

Because if you're not at peace with life
You cannot land firm in your cause
You can only do as dreamers do
Talk about one day and the pause.

Rice and Beans

You listened as I fell away
And I owe you all my life
I was melting like a milky way
And reeling from my strife.

I sailed the moon from yesteryear
And just dropped by to say hello
Had hoped you'd see some resemblances
But all I found was bitter ego.

I wonder if I didn't look this way?
Would my fare be held in place?
Or would it then come undone?
Like Mark and Mary Grace?

I figured you wouldn't come around
For folly is not your tea
But sitting idly on the bench
Is good ol' Captain C.

I warned of death and destruction
And we see it going on
Have we become numb to pain?
Just like Father John?

Or have we still a part of us?
That travels to the scenes?
Are we falling apart, my friends?
Or coming together like rice and beans?

Hocus Pocus

I'm tired of your silly games
Your politics are atrocious
You walk around like you don't know God
It's like you're under hypnosis.

I'm trying not to blow
But I can hardly control the prognosis
I'm on borrowed time
Just like *Hocus Pocus*.[156]

---

[156] Ortega, K. (Director). (1993). *Hocus Pocus* [Film]. Walt Disney Pictures; Buena Vista Pictures Distribution.

Kant

Now to gain composure
I'm running out of time
I haven't got the discipline
To stop this crazy rhyme.

I belong to another place
When family was all we needed
We'd play cards or race
We'd conquer the conceited.

But you today
You feed it
You crash around
Forget to receive it.

Like a birdcage
Always seeded
But your life is lost
Never completed.

Stay away from what's heeded
It might make you ill
Long for what's repeated
Remember "knot" to kill.

But in your wholesome travels
You can shame him all you want
Let him know you're onto him
And his name will never be Kant.[157]

---

[157] Kant, I.(1991). *Kant: Political Writings*. Cambridge University Press.

Slay

You can fool a wise old man
You can break his soul
You can make him vote for you
When you really plan his stroll.

But you can't hide your stage-cloth bash
It's quite the sight to see
You might win some along the way
But you will never conquer me.[158]

There is no way on God's green earth
That you won't pay for this
Your busy hands have carved too much
But what I have you can't diss.

You're afraid of me just like the rest
That's why you sent your boy
But to your surprise I opened his eyes
Before you could declare your "soy."

Oh boy!
Old friend, you think you're me
I created the role for you
While you practiced envy
Well, I see you want a divided class
Very unlike Jesus, very unlike mass.

But your sass
Is what gets them
The lonely bunch
Though they have many examples
They look to you in a crunch.

But I got a hunch
It's not going down that way
I got some omens on you
And like the kids say, slay.

---

[158] Hill, L. (1998) Lost Ones. On *The Miseducation of Lauryn Hill* [Album]. Ruffhouse Records.

That Cold

You evil, measly scoundrel
You found a way to divide the working class
You know they've long forgotten
The lessons learned at mass.

You know they're into identity
And stickers are well a bound
Though you've forgotten the body worn ones
That shield us from the sound.

I can channel your spirit
I need very little of your time
You waltzed in like a hero
Though you're really just like slime.

My paper written in graduate school
Is what brought you to sign
You think you're the "risen son?"
Better go get in line.

I am the one
Who can break your mold
You're as crafty as a citadel
And sneaky when you've sold.

But watch it all unfold
And you'll be the one to be consoled
Reach out my hand for you to hold
Lest your heart is just that cold.

Cinch

My children get so embarrassed
My husband tries to be a support
But everyone seems to know
I can't keep writing just for sport.

My finances are in ruin
Although I have three good jobs
I cannot make ends meet
End up looking like a bunch of slobs.

Yet, every time I try to stop writing
I'm directed to sit down
I need to channel for my ancestors
They cannot make a sound.

I sit in my computer chair
And the messages flow through my arms
I must pay very close attention
And listen for their charm.

He was here in this life
And thought no one knew his name
I was his granddaughter
And he never wanted fame.

All he wanted was family
And kindness in the air
Can't you find a way, my friends?
To show him that you care?

Or are you just that bare?
Like the shelves during a hurricane scare?
Always hunting for the rare?
But never acknowledging what you spare?

I know you cannot comment on my poems
I understand that fully well
You cannot tip your hat, my friends
I need you to act real swell.

This way when the day begins
You can be there in a pinch
I won't tell if you show up
I'll simply watch you cinch.

My Plan

The day has come and left us
But 13 years amount
You walked into my life as hero
And my heart beat jumped a count.

How ever did you find me?
I prayed with one candle light
Hoping you would show yourself
And then we met one night.

It was in Hoboken, NJ
At the Black Bear Bar & Grill
I wore a Navy work dress
You brought your internal will.

And by the time the night was over
I thought not once about another man
I knew you were sent from Heaven by
The one who helps me with my plan.

Grandpa Stan.

In Kind

Pasians, I have said enough
I trust you can move the boat
I haven't quite given it all up
But I feel the scratchiness in my throat.

Will you carry on the legacy?
Or will you take a pass?
I'm parting with my directory
And looking to make it last.

Fast
Like your life is dependent on air
For soon you will recall what it's like
When you have no one to care.

I'll be there
If you want, but only for a while
I have to raise my children
And you need to perfect your style.

I wish I could convey
Not to follow the crowd
But I know it's useless
You're all too proud.

But be loud
If you can cause it scares the devil man
Like when he was kicked out of Heaven
For plotting a perverse plan.

But man,
You follow the very wrong one
That dude in Houston
Is not the resurrected son.

Pardon my pun
But have you fallen and lost your mind?
You never charge for God's word
It's all in kind.

Front Runner

Mother Mary, I'm a wreck
I think you should move on
I know you've come for many years
Why not try Father John?

They think I am mentally ill
And I am not to be trusted
Rather look at pornography
Pin up the one they lusted.

How can I reach out to a group?
That clearly thinks I'm crazy?
Don't they know I work three jobs?
Or do they think I'm lazy?

No, they just see poetry
And think, "yeah, she's way off"
Never do they stop and think
She has a smoker's cough.

She has a smoker's cough
And yet she never smoked?
That must mean she's been around
And knows what's it like to be choked.

I won't say I'm giving up
For certainly I have an ounce
What I'm saying is will you join me?
In a jumpy house we can bounce.

I can guide your steps
But I need me a front-runner
I can be your muse, my friend
Show you how to be a stunner.

But you must all cooperate
And think without your mind
Remember the words I've shared
And always be oh so kind.

Mother Mary

The hands of time have come to pass
And I forgot my lines
I wrote 'em just as fast as I could
But then lost them in the vines.

I wonder if you'll call for me
When you've had enough
Or will you pridefully take a bow?
In the good ol' scrimmage bluff?

I'm sorry my words are so low key
I wish I could celebrate
There are so many good things here
I wish I could relate.

But my heart is stuck on a certain day
And I can't block it out of my head
It is the day of Good Friday
The day they pronounced him dead.

It plays within my heart at night
And makes my inner soul bleed
I wish I knew how to change its course
I could find someone to lead.

It's not a voice but an inner call
It's crying out to me
Can you avenge my son, young girl?
I think it's Mother Mary.

Never-ending Jealousy

Angel Gabriel came upon her
And said she would bear a child
She would call him Jesus
And his temper would be mild.

He would grow up watching Joseph
And learn about a carpenter's life
He would correct all the heretics at Temple
And they would cause his strife.

Never comfortable bowing to one younger
Never grateful to interact with thee
They plotted and planned to take him down
Our Jesus from Galilee.

But from the root of Heaven's magnolia tree
God flew down for his son invisibly
He took the final blow and Jesus fell to his knee
All because of people's never-ending jealousy.

Navy Seals

When you were but a wee one
Mother Mary held you tight
You were her most precious jewel
But soon became the cause of fright.

You were taken from her
And this fulfilled their plight
You were so wanted as a wee one
Because you bore her miraculous light.

Now flashback into today's world
And the same has up and happened
Some of Mother Mary's helpers
Became addicted to drugs and entrapment.

They forgot you were on loan to them
Their bodies gave in to the feels
But Mother Mary wants you to know
One day you will shine bright like Navy seals.

Yes, she is for real.

Sharp Comma

It's been a while since I wrote
I suppose you've given up on me
I wasn't able to hold it together
I exposed your entire tree.

I didn't mean to do it
I just felt I had to tell someone
What I found in you
Is worth more than the average gun.

You were a mere stranger
But honorable all along
I haven't met that many in life
Who could hold on, oh so strong.

I thought maybe if I impressed you
You'd show me a way to your profession
I don't know how to publish
I'm scarred from the resurrection.

If you find it within your grasp
To send me a lifeline
I promise to send you 200 poems
That can possibly pay the fine.

I have a bit of trouble trusting
And I don't have a clue of your loss
But if you connect me with a publisher
I will make good like a boss.

My poems are dark and windy
They're not flowery like an ocean's breeze
Do you think you can find a home for them?
Or will they blow away like a sneeze?

I know I haven't put much time into finding a path
I was hoping that's where you'd come in
I've written more than 200 poems
But don't know where to begin.

My house is in foreclosure
Though I bought a little time
I work three solid jobs altogether
But scarcely can I climb.

I can't seem to get ahead
No matter which way I go
Sometimes it's the girl at work
Others it's the "brave" Yugo.

My loved one's girls are suffering
That's why I am depressed
I can't believe my loved one
Took off her coat and dress.

For within her is pure evil
I cannot tell a lie
She clamored to her husband
She made him hate my sigh.

He tried to end my life
Three times of which I know
My loved one herself condoned it
She wanted to usurp my role.

Now that it's all said and done
Both adults got their karma
But there are still two children left
To deal with all the drama.

I wish I could protect those little girls
Give them all my armor
But I am only one person
Whose life is paused like a very sharp comma.

Invalid

Here is what you can do
I've said it all along
Use the persona I created for you
And infiltrate the dapper don.

Say you've found the one whom they seek
And watch them play my song
See how much you can get for me
I swear you won't go wrong.

Pretend you are my worst enemy
And you'll find the ones who scream
Understand the problem is
Nobody crowned our dream.

They saw him as a chameleon
And would not offer him praise
They thought he forgot the cardinal rule
You never upstage the phrase.

You must credit God
For each and every thought
That is why great orators
Will never hit the spot.

But the other issue was the message
Did Malcom make more sense?
Don't we need to protect our appendages?
Or have we lost all innocence?

I understand it is not my place
To choose among two great leaders
But I ask you all to read some academic works
And see if you can find the cheaters.

If you long for authenticity
Then you've found yourself in the right place
But if you're out to spew your mess
Then you'll fall like a big disgrace.

Always remember my voice it cracks
And that is how you tell my soul
I will never be a famous President
I'd rather die alone in a hole.

To know all they work to destroy
As you all cast your ballad
Never knowing at the end
They'll die morally broke, invalid.

Steal

Memories long forsaken
Is what I strive to reveal
Hoping that you'll tap in
As I remind you how to feel.

It's so easy to conceal
Pretend you are so real
But like the shiny seal
I'm the one they wish to steal.

Recorders

Now settle down, settle down
To all of my supporters
I'm not leaving that soon
I have to raise my two daughters.

But I slaughter
Anyone that takes an order
Turns around to call headquarters
Wishing for rigor mortis.

For my community is one without borders
Though I understand all it taught us
We need to keep close like hoarders
Lest we all get played out like recorders.

Mr. Lost

Arrange in small to larger order
Facilitate a brand-new flow
Rid the world of bullying
But understand why they sow.

Ask the man who holds the seat
"Can you out-write 'the one?'"
He'll humor at the suggestion
But never pick up the pun.

For deep inside he knows that he
Is nothing but fugazi
I'm rocking nauseous sips away
While he's fighting to drive me crazy.

But he can't hold a candle to my writing
I'm connected to the source
All he can do is have the audacity
To proclaim himself Mr. Lost.

Excessive Force.

Plant

The servant man could wake up
The gerrymandering could stop
But you're so used to inhaling it
It's like your frozen pop.

It's hegemony, friendlies
It's born and bred of wealth
It tried to snatch Nonna Tina
Proving he is stealth.

Well, I wouldn't let you have her
I wrote and wrote my song
This way the lives in purgatory
Know how to be strong.

The sour patch is ready
It's working for the grant
Hoping your day is a good one
It's that seed you forgot to plant.

Lock

Your tidying has made you reckless
Your humming has made you switch
Your lying thoughts are endless
Like bodies in a ditch.

You now hold the power
You now hold the key
But you choose to devour
All that makes you see.

You rather stay in silence
Protected by the veil
When the one for whom you wait
Can barely even exhale.

It's part and parcel roaming
It's fire in the vein
It's lollipops for free
It's what happened on the train.

I can't explain it all to you
My head is on the block
Was hoping you would peep my stee
And put them all on lock.

Pebbles

Like pebbles between your toes
You brush me off in a hurry
But one day you'll be looking for me
And it will all become rather blurry.

I gave you a chance to listen
I gave you a chance to decide
But what you don't know about next steps
Is that I might just step outside.

I need someone familiar
But someone rather strong
I know it's meant for a Jewish man
To say "hey, I've come along."

But where are all the Jewish men?
Have they all sailed the sea?
I *know* they're not the very ones warned of
Out there hunting me!

I'd say I'm a very fair person
And I am one percent Jew
Am I the one people wait for?
To avenge the entire coup?

Or are we looking to the sky?
For a man who looks like you?
I'd say the day of purgatory
Is held beyond the cue.

For I may not be that Jewish man
As I am a woman through and through
But until the day he shows himself
I'll be here writing to you.

I Am Boss

Think of what would happen
If you were crucified
Would you come back happy?
Would you find a way to confide?

Would part of you feel a bit lonesome?
Since no one stopped the display?
Everyone sat in horror
And watched them whip your beret.

Do you think you would feel certain?
Or perhaps a little bit upset?
All the people had to do
Was choose the one to set.

Well, choose is what you all did
You did it without regret
Now centuries have gone by
And not one of you even fret.

Well, let me be the first to say
If I were he, I think I would blow!
To see 2,000 years go by
And you're still pretending for the show?!

Meanwhile they stay steady chasing him
The one you put on the cross
Yet, you all sit and drink your drink
Complaining about the sauce.

Never ever have you looked around
And thought: "man, where is the toss?"
Like I declared in another poem
Only the true evil know that I am boss.

Embrace

Robert, they have found me
I cannot tell a lie
I cannot say I am the I am
For that would make me cry.

So, what do I do about it?
I simply write to you
Tell you all the petty games
Let you see what I've been through.

I haven't many special powers
Though I do have a few
They're useless in the board room
They're dangerous from the pew.

But I can't be a leader
For I am just a mom
Sitting here trying to connect
Before we feel the bomb.

My life is like a psalm
Praying you right the wrong
For it's as corrosive as motor oil
Deadly as this song.

You think your life is plenty
You think your life is full
But you don't know what's coming
It will whisk you away life a daffodil.

So, stick with how we grew up
But make it a friendlier place
Diversity does not belong to one group
You need it for this embrace.

Steer

I heard you thumping after midnight
It was your way of sending a sign
Your familiar walk in the morning
Lets me know that you are fine.

I remember your small apartment
Where you let us stay
I remember all the things you did
To take my tears away.

I know you love your daughter
But also understand she is tough
Like the waters in a few days
Some will see just how rough.

But I wonder if you know
How much I love and miss you
You were my tough nonna
You stuck by me through and through.

I'm sorry I exposed the family
I just couldn't hold it in
It eroded all my insides
Like tonic to some gin.

I had to express the emotion
Lest someone think it fear
Childhood must be a safe haven
Good parents ought to steer.

Conceited

You want to stop my writing
It's driving you insane
You want me to stop making you feel
You're starting to grasp my pain.

I'm sorry to bring you into it
But your words are sorely needed
If you can't be vulnerable in print
Then you must be conceited.

Class

You're not a partridge in a pear tree
I'm sorry to break the news
I'm the one you've been waiting for
But I always have to run from the pews.

The Catholic leaders know of me
And rarely am I welcome
It's quite a racket what they have
But some are really wanting hell to come.

You cannot trust anybody
Who hoards money when people are dying!
You cannot trust a country
Whose very role is to leave me crying!

The gray are not of this world
They roam from above the sky
I can tell them apart quite well
They have diamonds in their eye.

Behind odes of mass destruction
They seek to inflame your soul
They want you all in pieces
They want to break you whole.

The host is a mighty metaphor
Recall the steps at mass
Use them as set of books
And take them back to class.

Bored

My intuition is telling me
I need to clear the air
What my family did to me
Was most certainly that unfair.

But the lesson is not to sit and judge
For the lesson is to act
And for the record there are worse than them
They plot and plan my attack.

The culprits are from a land away
They clock me with their looks
Columbia's Director sold me out
To a certain bunch of crooks.

My family had no clue
Because they're self-consumed
But you all should have pulled the rug
Stepped to them as would the fumed.

Instead, you served and poured your wine
Even bought glasses so fancy
But Halloween has come and gone
While they search for the brother of Nancy.

Well, I am really not about to tell
But I have me a pass that's fair
It is to a Coptic Christian man
For all that happened there.

Make no mistake the man I see
He's not your average push over
He is a man who learned how to wait
And master the game of red rover.

Tell this man he has some friends
But also, many very bad forces
He needs to know the "I am saved" crew
Pursues him as one of the sources.

They make fun of us for consuming the host
And say how silly is what you believe
They got in many Catholic ears
And prompted them to leave.

They took my poem and published it
But in the form of a book
They made a fortune from my hand
While you all stood there, shook.

Don't you know it's a holy war?
That we have found ourselves in?
You must now hunker down
And remember what happened to Bin.

They look for certain religious leaders
The ones who could strike a chord
While you all sit and drink your drink
Saying "gee, why am I so bored?"

Weathered

Your searing thoughts are rescued
They've found another light
It doesn't mean I can't hear you
It just means you have to fight.

The world is full of danger
Anger is running fierce
But if you can change direction
You can find the heart to pierce.

And when that heart is ready
It will pump with every blow
Until it sees the real me
Then it will take it slow.

Such is what happened that fateful day
Grampa stood up and remembered
We have a past full of mystery
And no one is better weathered.

Rhyme

The moral of the story is
Be careful when you judge
You never know what someone's going through
You never know why they can't budge.

But if you see something going awry
Surely you can reach in
Lest you end up like petticoats
Covering up your own skin.

I hope this message reaches you
I haven't very much time
If the spirit moves you, my friend
Feel free to share your rhyme.

Foe

When you're sitting in a ball of flames
And you weren't saved for your sin
Think of this conversation
Think of what you did to your kin.

And remember you had many choices
You could have lifted the mood
But you chose to laugh and drink
You chose to let it brood.

You post very nice pictures
For certainly, I do as well
But one thing I don't do
Is pretend you're not to hell.

For I might not be as stable
But I know right from wrong
That's why my fan club
Sings me a damn good song.

I know how to turn it off
I know when to let you squirm
But one thing I don't know how to do
Is say it any other way than firm.

What you did was wrong
Yet, you post about Martin Luther King?
You turn a blind eye to injustice?
Yet, you take pictures of yourself on knee?!

That's a very big problem
For all you do is for show
Let's see what you become in your next life
I'd say you'll always be a foe.

The Man up in the Sky

Now step outside your comfort zone
And place yourself in my shoes
My mother made me sickly
My stepfather cried the blues.

They wanted to see me disabled
They wanted me to collect a check
They wanted to control my bank account
They wanted to see me a wreck.

To all my extended family
You watched this all unfold
My mother's mental illness
Is something you never consoled.

You found yourself quite lucky
In that it wasn't you
Never thinking "what about the children?"
Your apathy has shown right through.

So, if I haven't seen you
It means you're out of grace
You never bothered to protect me
You'd rather win the race.

But to your horror I survived it
While you all say "how sad"
You sacrifice your family
To follow every fad.

So, when your day is upon you
Recall this chilling time
The door is open for you
To confess your sin in rhyme.

But if I do not see of you
I'll know you truly don't care
Better off going to the beauty salon
Talk to the girl who does my hair.

Never did you consider
That when you turned your blind eye
You'd be disrespecting Jesus
And the man up in the sky.

Take your Places

So, let's face it
My life is like running bases
Channeling back and forth to different places
So, I can deliver you to all aces.

But you make fun of different races
When you need to unite diverse faces
Before this world erases
Everything the man disgraces.

Take your places.

Down with the Hood

Twenty some years ago
A professor wrote about Jersey City[159]
Said firefighters and kids were racist
Offered not one thing pretty.

Ask her if they can carry
45 pounds of equipment
Save one who looks nothing like her
Hold them a mile on the cement.

It's not my place to see if she's done it
It's not my place to see if she cares
But what she said about Jersey City
Was most certainly that unfair.

Never could she command the trust to sit down
And ask "what's truly bothering you?"
When I do the asking, I hear how their pop's not around
And their mom is out for the screw.

Sure, they might blame "minorities" to *you*
But it's because they think that's what you want to hear
We never told outsiders we got along
They'd break us apart with their shear.

Does your eagerness to absolve your own privilege?
Make you say they cared about historic white status?
We poor folks in the city
Just care about outwitting your elitist apparatus.

Funny how you published in 1999
Not too long before 911
Yet, you never rescinded your claim about racism
Even after they saved folks from every part of Heaven.

Let me ask you a question

---

[159] Fine, M. (1999). *The Unknown City: The Lives of Poor and Working-Class Young Adults*. Beacon Press.

Given all your PAR work?[160]
Did you share this book with Jersey City subjects?
Or did you leave them in the lurk?

I'm gonna go with the latter
And guess you didn't give them that modicum of decency
You'd rather call them deplorable
Than offer their deep stories as a peace entry.

Jersey City kids talk tough out of survival
But that's not a thing you would know
Still, I'll watch you continue to perform
"Down with the hood"[161] your only show.

---

[160] Fine, M. (2010). An epilogue, of sorts. In *Revolutionizing Education* (pp. 221-242). Routledge. See also Stoudt, B. G., Fox, M., & Fine, M. (2012). Contesting privilege with critical participatory action research. *Journal of Social Issues, 68*(1), 178-193.

[161] For a discussion of ethical issues such as deceit in participant observation, please see Erikson, K. T. (1966). A comment on disguised observation in sociology. *Social Problems., 14*, 366. See also Fine, G. A.(1993). Ten lies of ethnography: Moral dilemmas of field research. *Journal of Contemporary Ethnography, 22*(3), 267-294. See also Leo, R. A. (1996). The ethics of deceptive research roles reconsidered: A response to Kai Erikson. *The American Sociologist, 27*(1), 122-128.

Magician

There is little hope for the pig-headed
They simply refuse to listen
They steal shimmer from the sunroof
Just so their own skin can glisten.

But I stay wishing
For the day that one good Christian
Shows them what they've been missing
Takes them down the road of reminiscing.

I'm on a mission
To prove what they've been dissing
Because they're in fierce competition
With the one who once went fishing.

I'm a magician.

Password

Rarely have you heard a bird
As forcefully as I chirp
But the more dense and dumb you act
The more I get kicked to the curb.

You're absurd
You think I'm writing to be a nerd?
I'm trying to get the truth heard
But you're stuck on whether it occurred.

Friend, it's been blurred
Like Miss Muffet counting her curd[162]
He whispers to get me murdered
While you change your daily password.

---

[162] Bornstein, H., & Saulnier, K. L. (1992). *Nursery Rhymes from Mother Goose: Told in Signed English.* Gallaudeuizt University Press.

Envelope

He's as morbid as the midnight
He studies those without hope
He longs to see how religion
Can save some from the rope.

But he simply cannot cope
He took me for a dope
And now he's slipping like soap
Trying to prepare his envelope.

Guilt

Guilt weighs a thousand pounds
Rarely do some feel its emotion
But it lives within Catholic Christians
And it causes major expulsion.

Guilt weighs a thousand pounds
It even has a trademark walk
Some are slow and staggered
While others bounce around with excessive talk.

Guilt weighs a thousand pounds
I notice it from all around me
Some are very shady in their ways
They extend their necks to inspect the dowry.

Guilt weighs a thousand pounds
Some walk around with the shakes
Never sure how to resolve it
They turn to drugs and avoid funeral wakes.

Guilt weighs a thousand pounds
I bear plenty of its harm
Would I still have my family?
If I didn't upstage the charm?

Guilt weighs a thousand pounds.

Grieve

How do you grieve?
Is it with the heart of a broken child?
Or is it with a brave, still face?
Is it with the most postured smile?

How do you grieve?
Is it with tears that pity follows?
Or is through your anger?
That your soul gives in to wallow?

How do you grieve?
Is it with a wreath on a gravestone?
Or is it through the depths of hell?
You try to reach one on a pay phone?

How do you grieve?

Do Not Weep for Me

Do not weep for me at my funeral
For I am here in this life
Still, I don't meet Society's vision
Of what a good Catholic is in strife.

Do not weep for me at my funeral
I will never leave your side
Part of me will stay here with you
For, you've now got my voice inside.

Do not weep for me at my funeral
I need to fulfill a higher calling
All I ask is you help my children
Cannot stand to see them balling.

Do not weep for me at my funeral
My spirit has gotten too heavy
I can't carry it around anymore
It's weighted by adversary.

Do not weep for me at my funeral.

Your Funeral

I will not weep for you at your funeral
I will raise you into my arms
You are my great-granddaughter, Genueva
I named you from the start.

I will not weep for you at your funeral
You are a big girl
You've taken all they've thrown at you
And it formed your inner whirl.

I will not weep for you at your funeral
I'm the one who sent you there
You and I knew it would be difficult
But you got to feel Grampa's care.

I will not weep for you at your funeral
I will smile at your life
You are a proud masterpiece
Living under the most cutting knife.

I will not weep for you at your funeral
I will keep your spirit alive
I will make sure your children know
You were the one in the right.

I will not weep for you at your funeral
But I will play sad Catholic songs
Knowing that formed your inner core
How could any of us go wrong?

I will not weep for you at your funeral.

Skippy

Now we come to Skippy
That one must repent
He must be made to see
What he spent during Lent.

He must see his treasured goods
Placed in harmony
He must be made to choose
Which to bring to security.

But that will be a game you play
Never will you hurt a fly
You can hurt some other bugs
But those are not do or die.

They crumble as they lie
And after you will sigh
How two precious queens a nigh
Could represent the rye.

Oh my
You settled on my thy
You thought you'd make me cry
And I'd roll over like a spy?

Try
You're mistaken like some lye
Rub it in your eye
And see if you can buy
Your entry to the sky.

And then sis,
You come out with the diss
If you're the man, then cease to exist
All the ties that you once fizzed.

But his three wishes will he miss
For within them was a kiss
Only to hold if you're not remiss
Lest forsaken be their list.

Your Bed

I find your letter of this week
To be really out of place
For in it all you sought to do
Is make sure you won't be disgraced.

You don't want your reputation
To be tarnished as happened to mine
You want to go down as a purist
And one that is divine.

Well fine
I understand what you'd like
But where were you when I was down?
Must have been on strike.

So, I pass the mic
And ask if you want anymore
Heaven's out of certificates
But I can check you at the door.

I'm poor
In spirit but magically blessed
I'm like a lucky stripe
On your borrowed wedding dress.

I must confess
I held you on high
And gave you all your power
Meanwhile you plotted against me
Like a bottle of whiskey sour.

But I am power
Like no other
Even you must attest
For in my house, you worship
I permit you as a guest.

But dude, you are a mess
Your priorities are way out of order
Try watching your grandchildren
From a broken camcorder.

You slaughter
Your academic daughter
Within the big house
Yale is very sketchy
Like George, Lenny, and the mouse.[163]

What a louse
But I still hold on
For you were my cause
How to make a rich man
Care about the gauze.

But of course
You're not just a rich man
But a billionaire at that
You took money to avenge WWII
And that makes you a rat.

Well hun,
I got Nick's father Tat
All over your gat
That's why it never works for you
But your pockets stay fat.

So, let's chat
About what you want
Cause I know you're scheming
Wanna send me some money
Make up for the demon?

What happened to the sea men?
The Navy, you fools!
Don't they have an honor code?
Or should a Marine watch his drools?

Offer him water when he's thirsty?
But then take it back?
Like the giver he once was
He planned the attack.

---

[163] Steinbeck, J. (1994). *Of Mice and Men*. Penguin.

And yo, it was wack
You should have seen his bunch
Like kids playing Commando[164]
I ate them for lunch.

But one she packed a punch
She was a Korean girl
Warned me that his son
Wished to see me a swirl.

Well Pearl,
I got some hidden
Like the man with the cleft
He can carry on for me
And stomp on my left.

Cause yo,
I am one of the best
That you ever will see
Kiss up to my friends
Is what I will never be.

But he
Wrote the seminal piece about honesty
Rightfully lectured ethnographers about deception
Made them cry in their tea.

Only to then see
Just who was the one
Behind the hits
Better luck next time
Like the silly rabbit and his trix.

I switch
To my children
Cause I can multi-task
While your destiny is one
Of Carole and Bask.

---

[164] Lester, M.L. (Director). (1985). *Commando* [Film]. 20th Century Fox.

Why wear a mask?
Everyone will soon know
What you did to me
Not for pride or for purpose
But to scare the enemy.

And you'll see
What you threw out
Like a pistachio shell
I'm preparing your bed
And it will be in hell.
Oh well.

Well Read

I can't believe he did this
I can't believe how little he cares
I can't believe he sold me out
Like Goldilocks and the three bears.[165]

I swear
I never asked for much
Just honesty and some friendship
To help me through a crunch.

But you, you had a hunch
I was something more than I said
Someone you're afraid of
Someone you'd rather see dead.

Someone call Fred
I want him out of my head
I don't care for him and his crew, well read
Cause he tried to make my bed.

Well said.

---

[165] Brett, J. (2016). *Goldilocks and The Three Bears*. Penguin.

My Friend

The only care you have
Is whether I will publish your story
Cut you down to size
Make your reputation lose its glory.

I'm sorry but
You care only if your family could be found out
Care only if they'd be inconvenienced
Care only about your own drought.

You pout
Like a kid who lost his favorite toy
You play it up for the camera
Like the real McCoy.

Oh boy,
You are not soy
I am the one
You keep selling books
And I'll fight you without a gun.

Cause hun,
You're on the run
As you've always been
I play for keeps
While you kiss up to Ben.

My friend.

You're Shot

Like a guilty party
You arrive at the end
Were you looking for me?
My old and dear friend?

Wow, I comprehend
I've been through a lot
And you never offered shelter
Not even food that's hot.

Man, you are a snot
No more than a rolling knot
See you on the Serengeti
Watch you sleep on a cot.

You're making me hot?
I'll send your soul to rot
Put your head in a pot
On your cast I trot.

Cause you're nothing but a dot
Looking to connect to my spot
But I foiled your plot
So, now you can live life like a robot

You're shot.

Confined

Yesterday you reached out to me
After I don't know how long
And in doing so you gave me
The closure needed to write this song.

Everything said about you
Is entirely true
You did seek to have me branded
You did plan a deadly coup.

I just can't believe how little you care
Like my life isn't worth a dime
You could not write an ounce on me
I rep for the king of rhyme.

But now, I must take my time
And tell you you're a piece of slime
You're done pretending like a pantomime
You better go find you a wall to climb.

Cause I'm fine
But you're not looking too kind
I've sensed you in my mind
And you'll soon be confined.

I Stand

This tattered flag was all I had
I was left for certain death
But with this flag in hand
I wrote the play Macbeth.[166]

I'm sorry to disappoint you
But I am just a writer writing a song
I haven't got the gumption
To tell you right from wrong.

And I don't belong
This is not my true home
I'm just visiting right now
While they prepare my throne.

But I've been shown
A few things that you might not know
Like a baker's dozen
It started with the dough.

But I sow
All I want cause I aim for keeps
While you organize your pile
Of grocery receipts.

I sneak
Up and down
But I always come clean
This so you can select
Which one will talk to Jean?

I don't need a fien
I'm sorry but it's not for Kareem
It's for the one who can consume
A heart full of steam.

---

[166] Shakespeare, W. (2003). Macbeth. In *Teaching Literacy through Drama* (pp. 110-122). Routledge.

That is not one you can let fall
For he stole the heart
Of the Ivory Lord
So, I raise my sword.

And ask someone to catch up
Bow to my hand and
Drink from my cup.

My pup is too young
While you are of age
Registration is open
Searching for volunteers.

Don't fear
Come forward and
Show your hand
It can be in a meme
It can be drawn in the sand.
I stand.

My Own Song

Jesus, you gotta give me a minute
I know your heart is on fire
I wish I could take out what's wrong with them
Like lust and similar desire.

But I require
Someone whose reputation is strong
Someone who has not done any wrong
I need someone to step in for me
I cannot sing my own song.

God Bless

I understand you see me as blessed
But right now, I am stressed
I'm in a state of duress
Searching for someone to attest.

I want only to be the best
Help heal those needing rest
But I can't escape this test
Until I do confess.

I'm a mess
Took the life out of the devil's dress
Like the price of gas at Hess
I rose to the occasion of guest.

Waiting for the man called Les
To see if he can redress
All I said in jest.
God Bless.

Homage

I will not lift my sword against you
For I will use my flow
You're as cutting as an Axelrod.
And wicked when you sow.

You practice witchcraft every Saturday
You walk and walk about
You refuse to give it to me
You rather see me shout.

I am not concerned with them
Only if they hurt a child
Then they're fair game for you
And I wouldn't make it mild.

I will avert my eyes on cue
And you will know you're in
If I look away from you
It means you have some sin.

There is time to work it out
But that I wouldn't advise
Just take a look at those who have taken their time
You can see death in their eyes.

Karma is something outside my control
For it is pre-set like a locomotion
If you step on me, the angels step in
And give you that deadly potion.

It's sad to see it happening
But the proof is in the damage
If your life has turned after interacting with me
It means you owe me some homage.

Sociology

Sociology is a funny discipline
Within it are many fathers
Marx, Durkheim, and Weber
Can help us avoid the slaughters.

There is God the Individual
And he has shown his hand
Now, it is time to form "God the Collective"
For Footprints in the Sand.[167]

Think of a circle-like world
With dashes instead of solid lines
The spaces resemble faith
To be back-stitched into signs.

You're supposed to weave in and out
You're supposed to try your best
You're supposed to help your family and friends
You're supposed to take care of the pest.

---

[167] Hart, R. (2019). *Footprints in the Sand*. Retrieved from https://www.ryanhart.org/footprints-in-the-sand/

Looks

You're really not a friend of mine
If you can't open your mind
You're really not kin of mine
If you can't press rewind.

Learn from the Crucifixion
But not what they teach in books
Listen to what I'm telling you
Follow the one with the looks.

The Crown

Your silence is understandable
For certainly, I do not belong
If I had known this world would be so bitter
I might never have come along.

I might have stayed in my old camp
And played kickball in the street
I could have sat in my old apartment
And longed for the day we'd meet.

But something told me you're all worth it
Something told me to try
Something told me you'd see through this
And bat them another eye.

But every time I think I broke through
I find my will turned down
It doesn't solve the enemy's problem
It beats us to the crown.

Grand Slam

I grew up with wolves
You cannot shake my core
You can only run your game
And try to keep me poor.

But like the witch's snore
One day you will abhor
All you came to lure
Out the hood, old back door.

Like the Pink Panther[168]
Who gets tested daily by Cato
My family has put me through the ringer
When I just wanted play dough.

But when you are a special type
People sense you're gonna be tested
Best get you in tip-top shape
So, one day you can be well rested.

But I invested
My entire heart and my soul
I'm asking if you feel me
Or has your heart turned that cold?

I've been through major heartache
And lost my command
I've been sitting on the side lines
When I can bat a grand slam.

---

[168] Levy, S. (Director). (2006). *The Pink Panther* [Film]. Sony Pictures.

The Care

I am not afraid of death
I am afraid of failing
I was given a gift from God
When I was head over a railing.

I only wish you harmony
And truth beyond despair
I wish you peace and prosperity
I wish you to spread the care.

Happy Days

Why didn't you tell me about your trauma?
You simply never asked
You made an assumption about my privilege
You never considered a white person's class.

And now that I have startled you
Into seeing your own wicked ways
Perhaps you can give me a chance
And create some happy days.

Petty

They break your spirit when you're down
Instead of lifting you up
They make you feel you've done wrong
When you're really the best pup.

They're not proud of what I achieved
They think I don't deserve it
How did Jenn get ahead?
Her sister was supposed to swerve it!

Not unlike them "academia" nuts
They gossip over people
Never crediting God
Never visiting the steeple.

They think they're morally superior
Because they care for the elderly
Even though they take all their money
They still walk around fresh like celery.

I've watched several family members perish
After being "taken care of" really well
The beginning of their stay was wonderful
While the ending was pure hell.

The caretaker is by far the most anti-racist
But paternalism is his problem
Still, you all glorify him
Baby blues got you sobbin.

Petty is what they are
You can find them in any group
They look out only for their own interest
And care less who ends up in the loop.

But like the mighty hawk I swoop.

Scorcher

One day my stepfather
Must have been high on some coke
He pointed the devil digit at my nonna
Pulled her chair out from its spoke.

Instinctually, I moved behind her
She screamed for her niece, Adele
He somehow had the power
To send my nonna to hell.

He was growing antsy
Cause Nonna sat on her purse
But when I moved behind her
I saved her from his curse.

I absorbed it myself
Cause I understood he hadn't realized
The one who truly belongs in hell
Is one I dealt with, full of lies.

But on that day, Grampa called 911
And said he was acting violent
Funny, when the police showed up
He got ever so silent.

They asked Nonna what happened
But she wouldn't rat
She used to say "hate the drug, love the man"
With police she wouldn't chat.

So, they believed him as always
He had a convincing way
Calm after causing others to scream
He smiled as they watched his sashay.

The police called it the "coo coo" house
To describe all the frivolous calls
Though they suspected something was awry
I guess they didn't have the balls.

The police did not believe Grampa
And when I tried to back him up
The cop said "I know you're bipolar"
Made me sit down and shut up.

The police never have helped me
They've always made things worse
But I still stood up for them
When they were being cursed.

I suppose it is my optimism
I feel if they only understood
They'd change their procedures
And learn how to work in the hood.

Perhaps they would know about the games
The deep psychological torture
Some poor call one another crazy
And threaten them with a scorcher.[169]

---

[169] For a discussion of how families call authorities to take their children as a way of giving them a "time out" and teaching them a "lesson" (thereby exerting control over them), see Belknap, J. (2020). *The Invisible Woman: Gender, Crime, and Justice*. Sage Publications.

Man of the Hour

I saw him some five years ago
He came into the supermarket
His rage was taken out on the cart
His eyes loudly barked it.

He had big black Italian olive eyes
And seemed like one from around my way
But he was racing to the finish
He was pushing me out the way.

But I gained my composure
For I saw his tell-tale sign
He moved his phone from right to left
Back pocket to steal my line.

It showed me how it ended
With caramel leading the stew
It showed me there was hope
In reaching out to all of you.

In the end I beat him
I beat him fair and square
I met him at the checkout
And he gave me an evil stare.

He had to get certain items
While I shop on a whim
I let the spirit move me
While he looks to Mr. Grim.

Well, Mr. Grim, your time is up
Your chariot awaits
Just hope the dumps at Fresh Kills
Let you in their gates.

For you are a flat leaver
Far worse than a rat
You left your own family
You sought to tip your hat.

You traveled all over the world
You thought you had special powers
All because you saw some miracles
Seeping through my hours.

And you decided to devour
Take every truth and make it sour
You wanted me to lose my power
So, you could be Man of the Hour.

A Knight and Shining Coat

The unconditional love you received
Is about to take its pass
For you've abused the latitude
And taken it to the mass.

The sorry stand in refuge
While the indignant storm your boat
Mad the world hasn't brought them
A knight and shining coat.

But to the people who feel me
Let me say to watch on high
The condition is now in service
You can see it with your eye.

There is no place for hurting children
Especially in such a way
The folks that practice this evil
Must not see another day.

But like any usual matter
You must have irrefutable proof
Lest you sentence an innocent man
And find your life up in a poof.

Your Heart

Your parting thoughts are plenty
Your dancing days are slow
The fears you have are many
You don't know which way to go.

I cannot offer you reprieve
I can only sit with you as you cry
The code of where I come from
Means you always have to try.

Like the sighted man whose legs have fallen
You can see just where to start
But you don't know if you have the ability
To bring me into your heart.

Fair and Square

I hope you know why I've written
I had to put you on
I had to position you as an enemy
I had to save you and your son's bond.

The mood was catching up to you
And they were going to take you up
Like the contender and my 2005 email
I had to shake your cup.

This way they would think twice
Before taking you up somewhere far
Remember they search for perfection
And trap us in a jar.

Now play your cards against me
This way I will be killed by a friendly
Pretend you love me so much
And I'll be taken by the enemy.

This is the Durkheimian function of the batterer
This is the function of there
But now that you understand
Play it fair and square.

Surround Us

They go after religious people
Get that into your head
That's one reason China bans religion
Knowing top top comes crashing instead.

Communists try to protect their people
From the big bad folks who hunt Jesus
Never knowing how close Catholicism is
To breaking the wealth pie into pieces.

They go after Catholic schools
Because they think we think we're special
But they don't know how uniforms work
Every one of us experiences "mess hall."

We used to look out for one another
So much so that Durkheim[170] wrote about us
But his follower didn't like his findings
Wanted to destroy Catholic spirits around us.

They surround us.

---

[170] Durkheim, E. (1897). Le suicide: etude de sociologie. Alcan.

Communism

Communism is not far from Catholicism
Catholics are taught to stay low and humble
Never bringing attention to ourselves
We're supposed to blend in to avoid the rumble.

We take salaries that are below our worth
And that is to keep us directed
Never offering millions to the masses
But collecting it from those of us infected.

Communism is not far from Catholicism
We wear uniforms in camaraderie
To remind you about the collective
Never bowing down to individual pottery.

We value nature and working-class solidarity
Saving soldiers from certain fire
We go to wars when commanded
And only ask to one day retire.

Communism is not far from Catholicism
We don't get rewarded when we study hard
Told we must have been advantaged
When all we do is get double scarred

Do well in the University
And you will be seen as prime
As reward you get to work hard your whole life
While those who didn't study climb.

Communism is not far from Catholicism.

Their Breath

For all those who think they're superior
I suggest a few of several things
Take them to another country
And then cut off their only wings.

Tell them they have no heart strings
Let them learn a new language and how to sing
Tell them they need to get a job to pay for a ring
But jewelry is not how we sting.

Tell them they can come back to see their loved ones
Only after they pass the test
Will they change their selfish ways?
Or will they end up in arrest?

But remember this is all in jest
Help you think about a just pun instead of death
Let them work hard without the aid of meth
And see if that will clean their breath.

The Assassination of The One

Hey now, Mr. Skip and son
I'm glad we've had this talk
I know you could care less about me
And you'd rather I take a walk.

But what I've learned along the way
Is just how vengeance works
You dug your claws into my life
Then disappeared like one of the Smurfs.[171]

You told the FBI about my work
You told them I went to Al Tawheed
You told them I was one of your students
And that I must have met the wrong seed.

You told them I was a suicide bomber
And got me on that list
You made them break into my home
You wanted me to slit my wrist.

You encouraged me to work with Muslims
And congratulated me on a job well done
All the while you plotted against me
The assassination of the one.

I'd say that I feel sorry for you
But deep inside I really do not
You're a shell of a man trapped in a white van
And my wish if for you to rot.

---

[171] Hanna, W. & Barbera, J. (Executive Producers). (1981-1989). *Smurfs* [TV series]. Hanna-Barbera Productions.

Yale Tail

I knew about the RU screw
But didn't know about the Yale tail
I suppose I thought an Ivy league school
Wouldn't be as petty as a high-school scale.

But wherever I go is a trail
They show up as I begin to sail
In stores they follow me with a pail
They just want to see me fail.

The Drought

I never thought I'd say this
But my anger has settled down
I suppose all the expression of feeling
Has left me grieving for an empty pound.

I had to let loose my emotions
I had to let you all know
I'm not all together on the inside
But time will surely sow.

I've been through things of horror
As I'm sure you can relate
I had an army after me
But they've surrendered at the gate.

And so, I'll play civilian life
And see what it's all about
I only hope to keep my senses
And retire before the drought.

The Loop

I know I said a lot
I have the day after remorse
But I can only follow my heart
And it says to converse in morse.

It says that eyes are watching
It says that eyes are clear
It says that eyes are jotting down
All I say and do out of fear.

I haven't got the time
To organize a new religious group
I can only share my rhyme
And prepare you for the loop.

Cool Jenn

Now, let me gain my composure
For a meeting is coming up
I have to play cool Jenn
And pass it to my pup.

For my anger is ravenous
And will eat you up in one bite
I'm so sick of this twisted game
I just want you to make it right.

The Resurrection

For those of you not in the know
Here is the gist of what transpired
I was a graduate student at Yale
When 911 aimed and fired.

I know you think you know all about it
But trust me, you know nothing about this
Suffice is to say I met her at Columbia
And that lady did not sit.

She told her friends about what she met
Hillary Clinton and I even took a picture
She and the President worked it out
Before I could recite you some new scripture.

But as luck would have it
Yes, it's on my side, and that is clearly proven
The car bomb they put in my ride
Started smoking but only when I stopped moving.

I met with a "friend" around that time
And, true, he put me on
I knew the fuzz was onto me
Miss thing heard me sing my song.

So once the plan to swallow me
Was foiled cause the bomb didn't blow
They needed another plan to get at me
To kill me but disguise the show.

So, they tried to hit the Holland Tunnel
Make all of Jersey City fall under water
That was to erase the place where I was raised
Instead of sending us to the slaughter.

As luck would have it on the other side
Low and behold their plan didn't work
I was in the Holland Tunnel that fateful day
And since I'm a true believer, they're bombs can't jerk.

But to get back to the story about my past
Let me just tell you this
I wrote an ethnography about 911
And you may all read about it in my diss.[172]

You will see I strove to unite all groups
And show what we all have in common
But they didn't want that story to get out
They'd rather see you harm them.

I know who holds the current title
On reaching some common ground[173]
Perhaps my mentor tried to protect me?
From being taken upward bound?

But for me, it felt like a big let-down
Something bitter yet a little bit sweet
Like a powerful song from Adele[174]
My mentor and I would never again meet.

---

[172] Bryan, J. L. (2009). *"Terror Town": The Impact of 9/11 on Arab Muslims, Intergroup Relationships and Community Life in Jersey City* (dissertation). Yale University, New Haven, CT.

[173] See also Erikson, E. H. (1993). *Gandhi's Truth: On the Origins of Militant Nonviolence.* WW Norton & Company.

[174] Adele & Wilson, D. (2011). Someone Like You [Recorded by Adele]. On *21* [Album]. XL, Columbia.

The Fox

Now listen to me carefully
I will never steer you wrong
Some of you are afraid of Muslims
But trust me, they are strong.

They protected me from pure evil
They showed me how to roll
They accompanied me when they were after me
And to me that's worth more than gold.

They didn't know about all the hospitals
And I'm sure they would have been sad
To know the police broke through my door
Just because I wore the hijab.

To know that my own family
Were the ones to call me out
To know they agreed I was working with suicide bombers
To get me in a drought.

The only one who could clear it up
Would have been our man, Skip
All he would have had to do
Was call my stepfather or make one trip.

But he couldn't make one phone call
And tell him Yale approved the Mosque
For that would implicate his hand
And he would be seen as the fox.

So, what he did was let me fall
He watched them take me down
To know that my own family
Did not even see my crown?

So naturally, I looked to another man
I wanted to see if he heard me humming
Perhaps he could pseudo-adopt me
Like Arnold and Phil Drummond.[175]

Wow, after everything
The proof is in the running
Only my true enemies
Believed that I'd be coming.

---

[175] Grossman, B., Leeds, H., Hunter, B., Cohan, M., Brunner, B., & Hecht, K. (Executive Producers). (1978-1986). *Diff'rent Strokes* [TV series]. NBC; ABC.

Flip Phones and Plastic Bags

I'm back again
But I can't stay long
I just came to check in
And write you a song.

I want to tell you I'm with you
I want to tell you I care
I want to tell you I love you
I can deal with all the stares.

I'm here to rap this message
So, you can tell it's true
Not many people in the world
Can fix such a bad screw.

But I put my faith right in you
For I know you can heal what's broke
I know you can clear the air
I know you can reach out to the most woke.

I'm trusting you to do it
Cause kids are very lost
They're out there thinking I left them
Or scarred them as their cost.

They're thinking their race isn't favored
They're thinking their hair is unkempt
They're thinking God didn't love them
They're thinking they're exempt.

Well, these kids will have many problems
And not just in this life
If they can't spar with adversity
They'll never beat this strife.

So yes, you need to be sweet to them
Yes, you need to fluff their pillow
But if you don't teach them about me
They'll be wilting like the weeping willow.

Put your best on it
Just to make it fair
See how much of a dent they can make
Just how much do they care?

Can they reach out to the people?
Can they change their course?
Or will they fold like heretics?
Will they resist the use of force?

I can tell you how to do it
Of course, I've written many manuals
But I gave them all to Skip
Hoping he could rescue them peri-annuals.

But he's too busy with his legacy
Too busy preparing his clan
He can't help the lowly
He'd rather crowd them in a can.

It's about survival of the fittest
And they won't budge for naught
They believe the cream rises to the top
And motivation just can't be taught.

Well, let me say that I differ
I believe the people can do well
I believe you need to explain it to them
It's not something you can easily sell.

But as long as they know God didn't leave them
And that slavery wasn't alone to their kind
The entire world has cruelly had slaves
There was nothing bad about their kind!

We all have been through childhood
We all have been without power
Some of us may have had it harder
But does that mean the rest gets devoured?

That's sour
And something I can't condone
Get yourselves together
Before they send in the drone.

Listen to this word
As I am not just a Prophet
I'm here to help you understand
How to survive through the mosh pit.

So, stop it
I can't always hold your hand
I have to fight the demons
With the Rosary in the sand.

So, man
Can you please elevate my cause?
I'm not on parole
But I'm still feeling the gauze.

So, pause
And remember the goal of this message
Take care of each other
But don't let them win this visage.

I tricked it
I gave them a run for their money
But you don't stand for nothing
But getting your own honey.

Funny
I remember being there for you
But you bailed yourself out
When it come time to come true.

So now all I can say
Is you have a second chance
Do as I say or
You will lose this dance.

Organize yourselves
Diverse with dog tags
Lest you end up obsolete
Like flip phones and plastic bags.

Brand-new Way

I told you the day would come
When you would question my every word
The haters will croak like Peter
Before the rooster hits his third.

But true believers will stay
Diverse religious people will pray
Feds will ask some questions
While good police form a brand-new way.

Some Glory

I'll raise you to your silence
I'll praise you on your trance
But one thing I will never do
Is leave you in this dance.

You're part of my inspiration
You're part of this whole journey
Just think to yourself now
Would you leave your child on a gurney?

If we are made in his image
Then we know how our God rides
He's heavy on teaching lessons
He knows about playing both sides.

So why would you think he'd leave his son?
What kind of message does that send?
Only help your children halfway?
For they must learn to comprehend?

Well, that's not a good message
I prefer to tell my short story
But I wrote it to a bitter man
And he sold it for some glory.

Believers

It is, indeed, a sad state of affairs
When believers never thought it would happen
While non-believers counted on it.

Bum

Now for the heavy secret
The one I wrote to Skip
Jesus did not die on the cross
God came down and made the slip.

God exchanged his life for his son
Invisibly to avoid the looks
But this is not something
You can read in religious books.

You must decide if you accept it
The truth that God did not leave his son
He moved Heaven and Earth
To give you an example of the one.

But you let him carry a cross
You let him languish for hours
God flew down for his son
And in doing so gave up his powers.

But God didn't throw them away
He gave them to the Holy Spirit
This way Jesus could be whisked away
While Mary took their rod and speared it.

So, when you're asking why God didn't save you
And you're asking why no one could come
Remember that you killed God
And that's why your life is in a bum.

Brotherhood Secret

So, all in summation
Here is what they did
Invite a working-class young girl in
But make her pay the bid.

Let her carry the potato
Never catch it from her hot
Let her sit with all this wisdom
While her insides twist and rot.

Teach her about all the tragedies
That happened to all her kin
Let it eat away at her
Like motor oil to a glass of gin.

Like the history of urban renewal
Was not just to displace urban African Americans
They started this before with urban Italians
Made them fight like cold castle mannequins.[176]

Telling Italians they have Black blood
Getting them to feel irate
Knowing that what happens to Black folks
Would also be their fate.

They knew of the Italo-Ethiopian wars
When Italians got tossed out
They knew of the Italian invasion
And feared they'd end up back in drought.

They thought back to the lynchings
The ones Jean Scarpaci wrote about
That story got cold despite her dissertation[177]
They didn't want the brotherhood secret to get out.

---

[176] Gans, H. J. (1982). *Urban Villagers*. Simon and Schuster. See also Whyte, W. F. (2012). *Street Corner Society: The Social Structure of an Italian Slum*. University of Chicago Press.

[177] Scarpaci, J. A. (1972). *Italian Immigrants in Louisiana's Sugar Parishes: Recruitment, Labor Conditions, and Community Relations, 1880-1910*. Rutgers The State University of New Jersey-New Brunswick.

FDR gave Italians Columbus Day[178]
To make up for the lynchings the US ordered
Only to see protestors attack Italians
For cruel Native American slaughter.[179]

Politicians play games like quarters.

---

[178] Liestman, V. (1991). *Columbus Day*. Millbrook Press.
[179] Eason, A. E., Pope, T., Becenti, K. M., & Fryberg, S. A. (2021). Sanitizing history: National identification, negative stereotypes, and support for eliminating Columbus Day and adopting Indigenous Peoples Day. *Cultural Diversity and Ethnic Minority Psychology, 27*(1), 1–17.

Santa Claus

The voice of God is within you
This is what was said
When he read a paper I wrote
It practically marked me for dead.

They could not deny my writing
But they preferred to think of it as a cause
They wanted to send me away
Get rid of the hope of Santa Claus.

Second Coming

For those of you who say
"From whence is all this coming?"
I ask you to check your chest
And you'll find that Jesus is humming.

I know every family has one
A heart that's overrunning
With emotions held on high
Waiting for the Second Coming.

Abel and Cain

Yale knew all about the prediction
They even narrowed it down to clay
They felt "the one" would be a Sociologist[180]
Working on poverty and disarray.

So, they set up plans to spy on students
Record them in their play
See which one is most insightful
See which one could lead the day.

And then make a plan to devour them
This way the status quo can remain
And the rebels will fall down
Like the story of Abel and Cain.

---

[180] My argument here is that academics have been searching for "the one" who can heal what is broken and unite the working class. The one, by many standards, could be also thought of as "Jesus" or "the messenger." In my view, the one is a threat to status quo, not unlike what takes place in the film, *The Matrix*.

The Twine

Goliath is before you
And he's bigger than a tree
He's bigger than a bread box
Bigger than a university.

What you have before you is hegemony
Meaning an ethos that acts like a screen
You can't hardly penetrate it
Though you can see through the holes so clean.

A scholar by the name of Antonio Gramsci
Was placed in an Italian cell
The Fascists were afraid of his mind
Afraid of what he might tell.[181]

Well, he made many predictions
And one of them was just this
It will take someone working class
To rise to the top of the piss.

Someone who gets highly educated
Like at an Ivy league school
But then brings back all the knowledge
And teaches it to her crew.

This way the working-class movement
Can serve as a true grassroots sign
The elite can keep their money
But we will hold the twine.

---

[181] F.B. (2017). The strange afterlife of Antonio Gramsci's "prison notebooks". *The Economist*. https://www.economist.com/prospero/2017/11/07/the-strange-afterlife-of-antonio-gramscis-prison-notebooks

The Quake

The day has dawned upon us
And I must teach my class
Put in a full work day
And wrote poems for the mass.

It takes just a few minutes
But I must channel when I'm tasked
I can't ignore the spirit
Even though I've been unmasked.

Embarrassed by the attention
I prefer a very warm blanket
Curl up in a little ball
And pretend that I didn't make it.

But when it comes time to bake it
I can only say a truth that's naked
I cannot flower it up or rake it
For brutal honesty can never forsake it.

And I'll take it
Put my arms out and watch them shake it
But don't fake it
Cause if you do, you just might break it.

And we'll be forced to feel the quake of it.

Neapolitan

What are you? Is what they ask me
And they want me to pick an ethnicity
I'm a mutt in every sense of the word
So, I can't engage in your complicity.

One percent Jew, all parts Catholic
Once converted to Islam
I love all people and all religions
But my true soul is Neapolitan.

Sword

It was the spot in my tea
The sweat of my brow
The danger came alive
Like the soldiers of Mao.

It was the strike of my pen
The alarm of its chord
The way I carry myself
Thought I haven't a sword.

The Middle

Truth be told
I need me a pitch hitter
My cover's been blown
Like Jack and John Ritter.[182]

I just want to work
And be one of the moms
But nobody's picking up
The coat of arms.

So, I sit and I wonder
What will it take?
If you need some proof
Review the hospital tapes.

For there you will find
What they did to Jenny
Sent in men to kill her
Toss her out like a penny.

But within all the envy
Jenny saved a man
The man that tried to kill her
With the wave of her hand.

You could check the tapes
And form a conclusion
Reach out to Edward Snowden
And start the revolution.

Or you could stay grinding
And hope that your group
Stays way off the list
Of the smothering soup.

---

[182] Ross, M., West, B., Nicholl, D., Grossman, B., & Burditt, G. (Executive Producers). (1977-1984). *Three's Company* [TV series]. ABC.

And you might be safe
But just for a little
The game they play best
Is both sides to the middle.

Our Heaven

Even if you are guilty of naught
You can still say a prayer
Even if you didn't do those things
You're still guilty cause you didn't care.

If lack of caring applies to you
Then you've found yourself in the right place
Fellow citizens, raise your glass
And show us your best Amazing Grace.[183]

For she has to face each one of you
And always feel a fool
But she channels best at my command
And that you can't learn in school.

She doesn't want you to say a word
Or even note that you've read it
All she wants is you to organize
And figure out a plan to sweat it.

Captain D has a hold on me
Like fishhooks have to Leven
But brave young men could move the hen
And help us build our Heaven.

---

[183] Newton, J. (1779). Amazing Grace. In *Olney Hymns* (p. 53). Printed by W. Oliver.

Blue-collar Occupation

Heaven is a blue-collar occupation
It runs a lot like public service
One family can't afford gas and oil
Another family sets out to make a purchase.

Heaven is a blue-collar occupation
It's about evening out the rough spots
We ought not have drastic differences in wealth
We ought to share in God's lucky pot.

Heaven is a blue-collar occupation
But I have felt the true meaning of Karl Marx
He talked about exploitation of the masses
By the ones controlling the sorry shots.

Heaven is a blue-collar occupation
We can break and refix machinery
But what happens when we're kicked out?
We haven't any money to enjoy the scenery.

Heaven is a blue-collar occupation
And I can show you how it can best work
I just need a little breathing room
I'm being chased down like Papa Smurf.

Heaven is a blue-collar occupation.

They Plot

Friends and loyal family
I have an announcement to make
If you think this doesn't matter to you
Then you'll go down as phony and fake.

The game our academic friends play
Will most certainly affect your kin
Why, they've even gotten to Hollywood
It's a very deep level of sin.

They're behind assassinations
Of our most treasured leaders
They prey on college students
Those pesky dissertation readers.

All the while looking
To see if they can find the one
The one who could expose the bitter tooth
The one who filled in for the son.

And once they think they've found her
Man, you can't believe what they do
They try to drive her crazy
Knowing no one would believe on cue.

You want her to pay for not saving you?
Throughout World War II?
What if she were right there with you?
Aligning herself as a Jew?

What if she held your hands?
What if she were falling ill?
What if she stood in that gray horrid prison?
And gazed out the window sill?

What if she couldn't imagine how to stop it?
What if she could only bond with a few?
What if knew it was wrong to discriminate?
What if she learned that in a pew?

But Musa gave the Commandments
Though he forgot the dot
A period comes after the word "knot"
And that is how they plot.

Put up a Fight

I have always been here for you
And like promised I've shown you my wounds
I only hope you can use what I've shared
To help you shake loose what is doomed.

I need a new Catholic Godfather
As mine became a wealthy born-again and snubbed my plight
I need you to organize yourselves together
And this time put up a fight.

Short on Time

Elect someone whose hands are worn
To play the part of Grampa
We need our own moral lead
To recruit our friends from Tampa.

Realize elites aren't coming down
To help us with our grind
The Pope, the Class, the President
All seek to play with your mind.

Listen deeply to your gut
For that is where I reside
Follow their unspoken rules
But give no one a free ride.

If Jesus chose to live his life
As a most common man
There can be no excuse for us
We need to make a plan.

I can write movies for you
Show you which way to go
But they stay on top of me
And interrupt my flow.

I have three important jobs
My friends, I'm a bit short on time
This is why I take to poems
I can reach you in a rhyme.

The Steeple

Your song has played its course today
You've taken two from me
One was my cherished uncle
Another was my Grampa C.

But I will not retaliate
For I've got both lives right back
One is the age of ten years
The other was born for this attack.

So, sure you can brag to your friends
About how you stopped me from publishing
But the people listening right now
Are breaking out of your puppet string.

I care not about influencing your elite crew
I care about reaching my own people
And if it's all the same to you
I think it is time for the steeple.

Mine

Grampa, it's Jenny
I miss ya
I wish you didn't go away
I'm trying to pass on your legacy
But I'm branded like a bouquet.

I doubt anyone would listen to me
Although I still give it a try
Your example meant everything to me
And I can't even tell you why.

You're the most decent person
In the Universe
Far from the average soul
You picked me up
When I was a wee little one
And showed me how to roll.

And now I'm here missing you
And wishing you would send a sign
I need to know if I am screaming to the dead
Or are they really mine?

Score

I have no power to forgive you
I am only woman
But one day when you least expect it
You'll get a visit from Grandpa Stan.

He knows who needs avenging
Though he's been dead for years
I still see him here and there
He comes to calm my fears.

He gave me the updated Commandments
Which I needed when I was in a jam
He made sure I lost that job in Georgia
For that was truly a scam.

He brought me back to New Jerusalem (Jersey)
So, I could guard Grampa's stay
He knew I'd never forgive myself
If I didn't try to stop that day.

But as much as I wished to stop it
I knew there was a reason why
Grampa was killed for who he was
I saw it in Jean's eye.

Someone got a list together
And spread it like a champ
They found out through Ancestry
If a slave was once in their camp.

They sold that list to certain groups
And told them to even the score
Too bad they didn't realize Grampa
Was the one who once led the poor.

What a score.

His Scar

You're cold and callous
Smile as you commit malice
But you're only average
Whereas I am a savage.

I'll see you to your stash
Cause you raised the bar
Never see you as the one
Drive a luxury car.

But you traveled pretty far
To come shop the bazaar
Lost your sense of justice
Trying to beat out the Czar.

But you're not Julius Caesar
Though you were born on the tar
You gave up all your morals
Competing with the Jewish star.

Even your boy Bill Maher
Is starting to see the whole spar
Your mind may be made up
But your heart still bears his scar.

Plight

The universe is draining me
I cannot tell you how
My energy is falling
I wish to take a bow.

The silver rose to claim me
But I fought with all my might
Made a choice deemed unacceptable
He punished me for that plight.

Security Guard

I know a man from around the way
He takes his time to start the day
He sleeps quite late
But works real hard
He's what you might call
A security guard.

He's not always there when you need him
But my, when he comes through
You wonder what took him so long
Until you see his man, Lou.

He's not like your grampa
He's the punisher for him
He leaves no stone unturned
He rearranges the gym.

Do you know what his name is?
I do but I won't tell
I don't want you bothering him
He's busy running hell.

All the bad people
Who hurt the innocent
End up getting their karma
You didn't think they would repent?

You got your rules twisted
That was Musa and such
I can tell you the real Commandments
But they'd kill me tomorrow at lunch.

So, I trusted them to Skippy
But he's probably spent
Maybe one day you will realize
Why we fast for Lent.

And then when you look up
And see this brave man
You'll remember the good old quarter
You'll remember the slam.

And then you'll see Charles Joseph
Masterful without a wand
He makes it look easy
Like a ball that's been palmed.

Bellarina

I remember when I first met you
You were chewing through the gate
You wanted to come home with me
You wanted to be my top mate.

You whimpered in a high pitch voice
Until the man opened your crate
You jumped all over with kisses
And the man said this was fate.

I named you Bellarina
Bella it was for short
You were the apple of Pop Pop's eye
With kids always a good sport.

You didn't like being alone
So, Pop Pop took you in
I had to go to work
And wanted you only to grin.

My heart is breaking for you
And I know you feel our pain
A little Lhasa Apso
Is joining the land of rain.

So farewell, our little puppy
You were the best we could ever find
Always know you're in our hearts
And we will keep you on our minds.

Long Lost Pup

You're mighty strong as people
In case no one told you so
I'm proud of the men and women you are
And hope to see you when I'm slow.

I know I take no comforts
But I'm on a mission to make amends
The messenger is a little busy
And wishes you to comprehend.

I won't say I'm speaking for him
For that would be quite conceited
But I will say I try to be a helper
Until the bad man gets unseated.

I met my savior many years ago
And was enamored by his draw
He spoke softly but with precision
He was my sweetest Grampa.

He lived his life quite humbly
And never asked for much
All he wanted was his family
And he was always there in a crunch.

I wish I could share his life with you
Because I know his smile would help
Also, his country way of speaking
Like a dire emergency becomes a welp.

He inspired me to do all I can
To make people feel good inside
Unconditional love was his way
It didn't matter your creed or pride.

I wish I could take the pain away
When you miss someone you love dearly
I know it can be unbearable
Like the hospital that tried to sear me.

But one day when you see them again
You'll thank God that you didn't give up
You'll be able to hug them all
As you would a long-lost pup.

And just like Mariah Carey
And "One Sweet Day"
Boys will become men
And show us a brand-new way.[184]

---

[184] Carey, M., Afanasieff, W., Morris, N., McCary, M., Stockman, S., & Morris, W. (1995) One Sweet Day [Recorded by Mariah Carey and Boyz II Men]. On *Daydream* [Album]. Columbia.

The Pig

One day a bad man hurt a child
In the most despicable way
Jesus turned him into a pig
And the evil man went away.

But the people didn't want to stop
They liked treating children like sex-slaves
So, they said Jesus killed a good man
And that's the true reason he caved.

They sent in men to get him
And he knew they were on the way
But he had to live by the code of the land
Even if they were morally in disarray.

And so, they came to take him
And the Holy Spirit flew back home
God said stay still and wait here
While he set out to roam.

But the Holy Spirit couldn't sit still
She flew down to follow God
She felt something was wrong
Inside she felt something odd.

She showed up near the ending
But God had already sacrificed his clay
He jumped into messenger's body
And he then rose up to save the day.

What a way!

Charm

He told you he would come back
But you're looking to the sky
You think it will be that easy?
Then you don't know "our guy."

He came back as a civilian
So, he could walk right in your shoes
He gave up most of his powers
So, he could show you how to beat the rules.

He didn't want you to say
"Well, easy for you but we don't have your gift"
He wanted to show you how to move
How to beat Mr. Drift.

But you're so hooked on modernity
You've forgotten the good old farm
Dance like no one's watching
But never lose your charm.

Institutionalized

At least some ask the questions
About the shoe laces
Have you had yours taken?
Mine were in braces.

They covered my mouth and nose
With suffocating silver duck-tape
They tied down my arms
They made a big mistake.

I thought the Black woman
Would save the day
But she just shoved her long nails
Under my beret.

Then the Asian man
I thought he'd understand trauma
But he shot me in the thigh
Listening to lies from Mama.

So yes, you can ridicule me
And say I don't understand
My skin is not Black
But I have always reached for your hand.

You say I can't understand
Cause I haven't been to prison
Well, hun, pardon my stance
But you would never survive what I've been living.

Still, for the record it happened
More than 10 times
I might not have gone to prison *in this life*
But I have been institutionalized.

My Rhyme

Even after all the
Searing stories I shared
Some will have no problem
Giving me the keen old stare.

They'll tell me I'm white
And so, I must have privilege
Never mind day or night
They afford me no scrimmage.

They know nothing of history
When Italians were lynched
They can't connect the dots
On the Eastern Gold Finch.

They tell me my family
Volunteered to come on the boat
No matter they were starving
Took the food out their throat.

But you, you can't float
Your ideas on my fam
We are good-hearted Italians
Not the kind who beat 'em and scram.

So, make your demand
What do you want from me?
You don't own my life
Or the right to diversity.

But I see you want to try
To say I'm unkind
Like a master manipulator
You play with their mind.

But it's all in good time
Try adding some thyme
While you perfect your T-Bone steak
I'll be living my rhyme.

Thinner

I have more than one enemy
Just for the record
So, don't get it confused
Lest your life becomes that hectic.

I'm not into hypocrisy
As that's what they share
My enemies want me broke
Like the rides at the fair.

They know how much it hurts
To say to my kids
We can't afford it right now
Have to live on the skids.

They know that my children
Have seen the entire world
They know they've been reincarnated
From old souls into girls.

They know they deserve the best
Of what the world has to offer
But they try to kill their mom
Before she becomes a best-selling author.

Or perhaps even has her day
As a Noble Peace Prize winner
For the one currently crowned
Never went hungry for dinner.

In fact, he's a big sinner
Takes your heat out when it's winter
Increases the price of food
Just to make you thinner.

Chevy Novas

I hope you're paying attention
As I'm dropping some crumbs
Cause like Hansel and Gretel[185]
You'll soon be walking the slums.

They want you on medicine
So, you could be overweight
Less energy to take them on
They'll beat you to the gate.

They don't want you in houses
They reset the foreclosure
They want you in the projects
Driving 20-year-old Chevy Novas.

---

[185] Browne, A. (1981). *Hansel and Gretel.* Walker Books.

Hot

All in all, I understand
You waver in your loyalty
You rather select one that looks like you
Hope they will bring you royalty.

But when you boil tea
It does not always come out hot
It depends on the flame
And it depends on the pot.

Still, a lot
Has happened in this lifetime
I've been to hell and back
Just to recite this rhyme.

I hope you climb
After your dreams
Lest your life comes apart
Like mussels to some steam
You can take it to heart.

But before you forgot
Had your head all in my plot
Wanted to see me take a nose dive
Into Iraq.

Well, it's get skinned or go to pot
You can only make a souvenir
After my life has been swapped.
I'm hot.

Trophy

Friends and loyal family
I cannot tell a lie
They wish to make a Job out of me
So, they can spit in my eye.

Their inner blood is restless
Racing to the avenge the C
Can you reach a hand out?
Before I become a trophy?

Like "Many Men" by 50 Cent[186]
They plot to avenge the past
They come from all directions
Even shot at me at mass.

I ask you to open up your hearts
I ask you to listen to me deep
I may not look like you
But for you my heart does keep.

---

[186] Jackson, C., Resto, R., Branch, D., Perren, F., & St. Lewis, K. (2003) Many Men (Wish Death) [Recorded by 50 Cent]. On *Get Rich or Die Tryin'* [Album]. Shady, Aftermath, Interscope, Universal.

Juneteenth

I am not African American
At least not in this lifetime
So, I know I cannot say
I understand what this day is like.

But I can use my inner gut
And imagination abound
To tell you all how much I'm thankful
For what you've done for me this go round.

You see, there were many times
When I fell upon back luck
Lost myself a job
Got bamboozled by a duck.

And each and every time
Like clockwork there there'd be
An African American elder
Talking strong and tough to me.

Jenn, pull yourself together
You have kids who need your help
Are you gonna let some mean old snob?
Limit your life to "welp?"

Are you gonna let some professor?
Get the best of you?
Just because they don't have your talent?
And there's nothing you can't do?

These are some inspiring words
Whenever I got down
So, to Dr. Grimmett and Dr. Williams
I would to give you both a pound.

For when I was told I was too "working class"
And that I'd have to learn to be more like Yale
I was so incredibly hurt
All I wanted to do was bail.

But Dr. Grimmett told me
In no uncertain terms
You never let those uppities
Make you feel like you have germs.

You never let them hold you down
Or run you out of their school
You hold onto what your family taught you
And continue to make them drool.

And for your words, Dr. Grimmett
You are the one who made me stay
You said "Black folks go through this
Each and every day."

So, with that I felt empowered
I'm not letting them hold me back
They do this to good people
To get them off their track.

So, thank you African Americans
There are too many to list
I for one am grateful
You made it through the mist.

And if ever that day should come
That your freedom is no longer free
I hope you will always know
You can count on me.

So, on this Juneteenth Day
I wish you every bit of care
For I know it must be bittersweet
To celebrate freedom from despair.

Test

Like the film with Anthony Hopkins[187]
I need very little of your time
All I need is one glimpse
And like a meter I can read your mind.

I can feel your inner monster
I can hush your tightened chest
But I can't make you stop feeling
You'll need it for this test.

---

[187] Poyart, A. (Director). (2015). *Solace* [Film]. Lionsgate Premiere.

Pinochle

The game of Pinochle
Is quite the delight
It's a strategic process
From left to right.

It's quiet and humble
And it rarely boasts
It's like a gin don
On a bachelor's toast.

For in this game
You bid on the kitty
Wage your bet your card's in there
Like *Jumpin' Jack* City.[188]

You win the hand
You show your meld
You bury three
And the others are held.

The kind of player you are
Tells much of your story
I always bury junk
While Grampa buried glory.

For me it'd be two queens and one sick nine
For Grampa it would be three kings in a design
But fine
What I'm really trying to yell
Is do you save your point cards?
Or play them under your spell?

Hell

---

[188] Marshall, P. (director). (1986). *Jumpin' Jack Flash* [Film]. 20th Century Fox.

Come Together Strong

It was my nose that did me in
Reincarnated Lombroso noticed its slope
He searched for years and years
And was almost out of hope.

He sized up my protruding jaw line
He noticed the color of my hair
This is the true reason Muslims cover
It protects women from their stare.

At 21, I walked in confidently
With a low-cut black skirt suit
And he realized just who I was
Now, his plan he could execute.

He played with my emotions
Took my DNA off a glass
All at a home holiday party
His balls were made of brass.

He then used what he found
To get folks to chase me down
It started around 911
And I couldn't make a sound.

He called certain jobs I worked at
And told them I was to blame
For everything wrong done to humankind
They decided to fire the flame.

Just like they did in Egypt
When they got Muslims to kill Coptics
Showed them pictures of trumped-up plans
Made them feel they were being mocked and ish.

They do the same all over
Former Yugoslavia was no different
They get the people to commit atrocities
As they sip lattes from their kitchen.

When I worked at one such job
They came after me near the bar
But I was onto certain dude
I picked the one who came from the tar.

And they could not believe I left
Such a good one at the bazaar
For they thought I'd pick the blonde one
Who traveled so freaking far!

They wanted me to have a baby
With the man they identified
They wanted him to steal my child
Get rid of me with faked-out suicide.

All because they're obsessed with miracles
Like Rapunzel and Mother Gothel[189]
They think my children can keep them safe
They wished to strand me in a private brothel.

I was onto their games
But I had to take a leave
The fuzz was onto me
And I couldn't call the police.

Soon you will all understand
Exactly what went wrong
For now, I'll ask you to say a prayer
And come together strong.

---

[189] Grimm, J. & Grimm, W. (1812). Rapunzel. In *Grimm's Fairy Tales*.

Hoboken

He treated people like sick cattle
Crammed them with no air in close quarters
Vomit filled in for a carpeted floor
The stench of dead bodies lost to slaughter.

The children cried out for Jesus
And wondered when God would come
I saw him on a bus one day
He looked seriously at me until I grew numb.

He could not do anything over the top
As "top top" was in sight
Came down to find the "lucky" Jewish woman
Kidnap her and start her plight.

Pair her with various ethnic partners
See which one of her offspring could best fight
Told she abandoned them at birth
As they pulled crying infants from her arms at night.

She could not even kiss them goodbye
Her insides were beyond torn
This marked the beginning of the struggle
Fated to be born to a Jewish mom with scorn.

Some Jewish folks were seen as feeling too special
While some non-Jews hated Jews for being "chosen"
Everyone forgot about the resurrection
Except Mother Mary, torn apart like the sisters on *Frozen*.[190]

Welcome to Hoboken.

---

[190] Buck, C., & Lee, J. (2013). Frozen. Walt Disney Studios Motion Pictures.

My Calling

So, here is what he did
With or without the blessing of the star
He sold my family to a certain group
Showed up from afar.

Sent them into the hospital
Where I was laid up
Wanted to do me in
Like an old car trade up.

But then what happened
To your big man?
He ended breathless
Until the wave of my hand.

Yes, I pardoned him
Cause he was just a pawn
The real McCoy is a nasty parasite
Chewing up your front lawn.

And then what happens?
When they can't make the hit?
Their family is killed
With the drop of his spit.

Leave no witnesses
That is his balling
But he can't stop me now
I'm living my calling.

Jacks or Better

The game is Jacks or Better
But only trips can win
The inning is out of limits
And rarely can you sin.

But on that day, you feel the wind
Sail beneath your soul
You will know internally
That I am the way to go.

I cannot persuade a Christian man
I'd rather wave to him on the low
And tell him he is the only one
Who led to my final blow.

And so,
I raise my hands to and fro
Hoping one day you all know
Just why I had to go.

Joe,
I know your mind's made up like Rao
But I think you better show
Our neighborhoods how to flow
As we did in the ghetto.

For then
Not only will you destroy them
Deep within you will find some friends
Whose music comprehends
How amongst us we must blend.

I'm on the mend
But I need me a rear end
Someone with whom I can pretend
That I'm not Isa, your best friend.

Oh when.

Too Long

I didn't know what you went through
And now that I do, I'm sad
To know you looked to me
Because deep down inside you were scared.

I spent my whole life waiting
For someone to come along
Notice the hard work and sacrifice
Maybe give a few bucks for my song.

Never knowing it was you
Who would end up righting the wrong
Never knowing it was I
Who held on way too long.

Snow

I care about your soul
That's why I've written this book
Jesus did go after the hole
He came before the one with the crook.

I understand you are secure with your riches
But I'm concerned about your afterlife
Do you want to be a carpenter ant?
And work through every strife?

Or do you want to be an angel?
Who travels back down to your family?
Gives them messages in silence?
To avoid a future calamity?

If you prefer the latter
Then you must make amends with what you hold
You need not hoard your money
You need save the ones whose hearts have turned cold.

I don't care if you're also a victim
I know the cycle of violence[191] well
The day you cross over to oppressor
You seal your fate in hell.

And just for the lovely record
You can also oppress someone white
All you have to do is smother it
Watch it give up without a fight.

You can call that karma
But deep down inside you know
If you don't follow my very word
You'll be left out in the snow.

---

[191] Walker, L. E. (2016). *The Battered Woman Syndrome.* Springer Publishing Company.

A Boost

And so, the lonely shepherd boy
Has finally come home to roost
It took him many years
But he now understands "a boost."

It took some basic training
With a bit of threat thrown in
To show the man what he had come to
And he shuddered at the recollection.

Sometimes we must push our friends
Beyond their comfort zone
Sometimes we see things in them
They don't know how to hone.

It's at times like these, my friends
You must give a man a bone
This way you won't be caught off guard
When he calls you from the throne.

Al Capone.

White Trash

Last time I saw you
You left me freezin'
Still, I stayed like a puppy dog
Beggin' and pleas'n.

But now I'll see you outside
When you start fallin'
Blow your mind with the truth
Like this poem book by J Hourin.

Biggie came from the curtain next to me
Cause I blasted "What's Beef?"[192]
In a hospital gown he asked for a "pencil"
Read my dissertation and found the thief.

I write because I cannot talk
Told my accent is too heavy
I write because I cannot walk
Surrounded by adversary.

I write because I am not myself
Had to change my mother tongue
They would not hire me with such slang
Thought I deserved to be self-hung.

I write because I am hurt inside
And cannot begin to explain
What it does to my insides
To hear you all complain.

You think you know the lot of us
Us Italians you use for a laugh
You think we are not onto you
You think we deserve your wrath.

---

[192] Wallace, C., Myrick, N., & Broady, C. (1997). What's Beef? [Recorded by the Notorious B.I.G.] On *Life After Death* [Album]. Bad Boy, Arista.

Well, too bad you don't know us well
We fight with our own to defend your path
Maybe one day you'll realize
Why the devil still carries your stash.

White trash.

Family Photos

Grampa Charlie & Nonna Tina

Nicola and Filomena Piccirilli

Grampa Charlie in the Navy

Grampa Charlie walking on water

Grandpa Stanley and Daddy John

Mama Charlene (age 18)

Nonna Tina and Jenn baby picture

Jenn and Nicole Christmas time (age 4)

Jenn (age 3 years), Grandpa Stanley, and Nicole

Jenn and Nicole Holy Communion (age 8)

Uncle Mark at Van Saun Park

Jenn and cousins at the pumpkin patch

Jenn and Nicole in Grampa's pumpkin car

Jenn, and friends at class trip

Jenn (age 9) and friends 4th Grade Photo

Jenn (age 13) 8th grade graduation picture

Jenn (age 17) senior prom

Jenn (age 18) at Rutgers

Uncle Alex and Jenn (age 23) at a wedding

Grampa and Jenny (age 26) just after 911

Mama Charlene, Jenn (age 28) and Grampa Charlie

Daddy John, Uncle Mark, and Grampa Charlie (1997)

Jenn in Italy (age 33)

Jenn (age 35) and Nick in Little Italy, NYC

Grampa Charlie and Nick (2011)

Jenn (age 36) with Angelia – First Ash Wednesday

Jenn (age 40) with Angelia

Jenn (age 42) with Gianna

Jenn (age 47) with Gianna

About the Author

Dr. Jennifer Lee Hourin (Jenn) is a multi-faceted author with a diversity of experience teaching at the University level as well as leading applied, policy-oriented research and program evaluations and practicing restorative justice. Jenn has worked with some of the world's leading think tanks on issues of social justice such as The Vera Institute of Justice, The Center for Employment Opportunities (CEO), and the Center for Justice Innovation (CJI) (formerly the Center for Court Innovation). Jenn earned a PhD and Masters degree in Sociology from Yale University with a concentration in urban sociology, race and ethnicity, justice, and community building. She also holds Bachelors degrees from Rutgers University in Criminal Justice and Psychology.

Currently, Jenn serves as Senior Research Scientist with the Department of Children and Families (DCF) in New Jersey. She is working on issues of youth mental health, trauma, bullying, and suicide as well as police-youth initiatives. She also teaches classes on Justice and Criminology with The College of New Jersey (TCNJ), and consults on issues of University-Community partnerships with Marga Inc. Prior to these roles, Jenn served as Assistant Professor of Criminal Justice with Kean University, The College of New Jersey (TCNJ), William Paterson University (WPU) and New Jersey City University (NJCU). At CJI Jenn served as Principal Research Associate where she led a multi-site study on the commercial exploitation of children (CSEC) with the Office of Juvenile Justice and Delinquency Prevention (OJJDP). There she also worked to evaluate the implementation of reentry courts funded by the Second Chance Act, and a program on the unification of families involved in the foster care system. Jenn served as Director of Research and Organizational Development with the Center for Employment Opportunities (CEO), one the nation's leading workforce development and reentry organizations for formerly incarcerated individuals. There she worked to ensure that research and evaluation helped to enhance programmatic innovations, so as to improve the programmatic experiences and outcomes for participants in real-time.

Jenn is trained in both Restorative Justice and Healing-Centered Engagement (HCE). She leads peacemaking circles as a way to improve cross-cultural understanding and empathy. Jenn has published in academic journals and books. Jenn's ethnographic work on the experiences of Arab (mostly Egyptian) Muslims in Jersey City after 9/11 was published in a chapter called "Constructing 'the true' Islam in Hostile Times: The Impact of 9/11 on Arab Muslims in Jersey City." Jenn is a survivor of trauma experienced through childhood and adulthood, and her story can be an inspiration to all those suffering with mental illness. She is the mom of two children, Angelia and Gianna, and wife to Nicholas J. Hourin.

Made in the USA
Middletown, DE
05 September 2023